"Old Testament professor David Lam̶ ̶ ̶ ̶l's emotions as described in Scripture: God's hatred, wrath, jealousy, ꞏꞏꞏꞏ̶ꞏꞏ, joy, compassion, and love. This very readable book includes personal anecdotes, theological reflection, and exegetical insight based on the original language used in Scripture to refer to God's emotions. The application of God's emotions to the people of God exemplifies the pastoral side of biblical studies, and this from someone who does it so well."

Karen H. Jobes, Gerald F. Hawthorne Professor Emerita of New Testament Greek and Exegesis, Wheaton College

"As we read in the Scriptures, God has emotions such as anger, hatred, and jealousy, and it is difficult to understand these coming from a loving God. In *The Emotions of God*, we get great insight from David Lamb, who is not just a super smart scholar but one who truly understands everyday life with average people. So this is a really accessible and practical guide to the very big questions about God's emotions. We are created in God's image, and this affects how we gain understanding of ourselves as emotional human beings."

Dan Kimball, faculty at Western Seminary and author of *How (Not) to Read the Bible*

"I finished this book with tears in my eyes, since David Lamb's closing words echo the love of my own heart for the Scriptures that show us the love of God's heart—and all the other emotions there. Indeed, if knowing God better is the goal of attentive Bible study, then this book achieved that goal for this reader. And if a sense of humor counts as an emotion, then Lamb's cheerful sprinkling of his own surely reflects something of God's own playfulness, while helping us to take seriously, for the good of our souls, the range and depth of divine emotion so richly expressed in God's Word."

Christopher J. H. Wright, Langham Partnership, author of *The God I Don't Understand*

"I laughed, cried, and worshiped my way through *The Emotions of God*. With a deft sense of humor and touching personal stories, David Lamb invites us to engage deeply with the biblical portrait of God as an emotional being. For those who struggle with the idea that God could experience hatred, wrath, and jealousy, this book will reveal how even those more negative emotions express the depth of God's love. And it will draw readers to worship God holistically—with mind, heart, and soul—embracing the emotions that God has given us as people created in his image."

Brittany Kim, Northeastern Seminary at Roberts Wesleyan College

"Many Christians fear their emotions. They worry their emotions will control them and make them do or say something they will regret. In his excellent and highly readable book *The Emotions of God*, David Lamb reminds us that emotions can be 'normal, natural, even divine.' After all, he shows us, God has a rich emotional life himself. Those who read this book will grow not only in their understanding of God but also of themselves."

Tremper Longman III, distinguished scholar and professor emeritus of biblical studies, Westmont College

"'Well obviously God doesn't have feelings. That would make him unpredictable and irrational. The Bible's just making allowance for our way of seeing things when it describes him that way.' Once again David Lamb shows how wrong we can be about the Bible (and God) and how much more interesting the Bible is than we thought (and how much more interesting God is)."

John Goldingay, professor of Old Testament at Fuller Theological Seminary and author of *Old Testament Ethics*

"We need this book because so many today are afraid or uncomfortable with God's emotions that stand up and shout at us. All over the place. Theologians have concocted an unemotional (impassible) God, but that God is not the God of the Bible. David Lamb has patiently examined seven emotions of God, and he has done so in the context of ancient and modern discussions of feelings. What we discover is that our discomfort is not God's: our God is an emotional God, and those divine emotions can become our instructors for our feelings. A must-read."

Scot McKnight, professor of New Testament at Northern Seminary and author of *A Church Called Tov*

"*The Emotions of God* is a deep dive into our Creator's heart and makes the case that emotions are both human and divine. It echoes the call to image our Creator by owning our own emotions and stewarding them in ways that reflect his heart for the world. Definitely the kind of wisdom we all need in these emotionally turbulent times."

Carolyn Custis James, author of *Half the Church* and *Malestrom*

the emotions of god

*Making Sense of a God Who
Hates, Weeps, and Loves* / DAVID T. LAMB

An imprint of InterVarsity Press
Downers Grove, Illinois

InterVarsity Press
P.O. Box 1400 | Downers Grove, IL 60515-1426
ivpress.com | email@ivpress.com

InterVarsity Press® is the publishing division of InterVarsity Christian Fellowship/USA®. For more information, visit intervarsity.org.

All Scripture quotations, unless otherwise indicated, are taken from The Holy Bible, New International Version®, NIV®. Copyright © 1973, 1978, 1984, 2011 by Biblica, Inc.™ Used by permission of Zondervan. All rights reserved worldwide. www.zondervan.com. The "NIV" and "New International Version" are trademarks registered in the United States Patent and Trademark Office by Biblica, Inc.™

While any stories in this book are true, some names and identifying information may have been changed to protect the privacy of individuals.

Author photo by Robert Thompson
Figure 1.1. Emotional wheel by Robert Plutchik / Wikimedia Commons, public domain

The publisher cannot verify the accuracy or functionality of website URLs used in this book beyond the date of publication.

Cover design and image composite: David Fassett
Interior design: Jeanna Wiggins

ISBN 978-1-5140-0010-6 (print) | ISBN 978-1-5140-0011-3 (digital)

Printed in the United States of America ∞

Library of Congress Cataloging-in-Publication Data
A catalog record for this book is available from the Library of Congress.

29 28 27 26 25 24 23 22 | 9 8 7 6 5 4 3 2 1

dedicated to

the memory of my dad and mom,

Dick and Jane Lamb

contents

I

emotions are divine

The works of the flesh are . . . enmity, strife, jealousy, fits of anger
. . . but the fruit of the spirit is love, joy, peace, patience, kindness.

GALATIANS 5:19-20, 22 ESV

WHEN WAS THE FIRST TIME YOU REMEMBER CRYING?
For me, I was nine.

I was watching *Brian's Song*. The made-for-TV movie (1971) was based on the true story of two Chicago Bears running backs, Brian Piccolo (James Caan) and Gale Sayers (Billy Dee Williams).[1] Despite obstacles of race and a running back rivalry, their friendship blossomed as they became not just teammates, but the first interracial roommates in the history of the NFL. Piccolo helped Sayers recover from a knee injury, but after Sayers' recovery Piccolo began to struggle physically. Eventually Piccolo was diagnosed with terminal cancer.

After Sayers is given "The Most Courageous Player" award, he declares, "I love Brian Piccolo, and I'd like all of you to love him too. And tonight, when you hit your knees, please ask God to love him." Piccolo died shortly afterward at age twenty-six. I wept at the tragedy of a life cut short by cancer.

Since ABC rebroadcast the movie every year, I annually repeated this ritual of tears. But I was always embarrassed about getting emotional, so I would turn away from any family members watching with me. If there was a blanket or pillow handy, they were used as barricades to prevent my tears from being seen by my two brothers. Unfortunately, uncontrollable sobbing makes covert weeping difficult.

Why did I attempt to hide my tears? I'm not sure, but I know I didn't like the feelings associated with tears—weakness and vulnerability. I don't remember my father expressing much emotion, and I hadn't seen many examples of men crying. Things have changed a little in the past five decades in terms of public expressions of emotions, but in many contexts, emotions are viewed negatively, and this perspective impacts how we view our emotional God.

"LOUD CRYING HE MAKES"

"Away in a Manger" is one of the most popular Christmas carols. I may not need to remind you of the words, but I will anyway, just for the second verse.

> The cattle are lowing, the baby awakes,
> But little Lord Jesus, no crying he makes.
> I love thee, Lord Jesus, look down from the sky,
> And stay by my cradle til morning is nigh.

Why doesn't baby Jesus cry? The cattle are lowing (mooing), so bovine bellowing seems to have woken him. What do babies do when they are woken up on the middle of the night? They cry . . . unless, apparently, they are divine. While I don't remember it, I'm pretty sure I cried as a baby long before watching *Brian's Song*.

While the biblical text is silent on any possible nocturnal noises that may have been uttered by the little Lord Jesus, the carol's lyricist silences him, depriving him of any emotional outburst.[2] It is difficult to determine the reason an infant cries. Hunger may be a factor, but emotions such as fear, anger, or sadness are often a primary cause—a child often calms down when comforted, even before being fed. If the Gospel writers provide us no hints about the behavior of baby Jesus, why do we sing that he didn't cry? I think it goes back to our view of God. We aren't comfortable with an emotional God. It's unsettling.

If people didn't find the portrayal of the stoic swaddled Savior compelling, this carol wouldn't be so popular. Emotions were deemed beneath baby Jesus, not just by the carol's lyricist, but by the millions of Christians who love and sing this song every Christmas.

While I believe that, like all human infants throughout history, baby Jesus cried, I don't want to ruin this song for people. My goal isn't to stop carolers from singing it, but merely to question what it implies about emotions and appropriate divine behavior. As we'll see throughout this book, the God of the Bible often expressed emotions. Big Lord Jesus cried on at least two occasions (Lk 19:41; Jn 11:35), and, according to Hebrews, he was even known for weeping (Heb 5:7). As a man who cries regularly (twice publicly in the past two weeks—in the Covid spring of 2020), I find great comfort in the image of a Savior who weeps, as an infant or as an adult. We are called, after all, to follow Jesus (Mk 1:17; 2:14; 8:34). Sometimes this will involve weeping.

Our God is an awesome God, and part of his awesomeness is his emotional-ness. Emotions are divine. Just as we have needed to update the archaic language of many classic hymns, this carol is due for a slight revision.

The cattle are lowing, the baby awakes,
So little Lord Jesus, loud crying he makes.

That's better. He's little but makes a loud noise—lungs worthy of a future preacher.

The negative perspective on divine emotion of this carol is tragically not unique. If it were, we could dismiss it as an anomaly. But many Christians, including biblical scholars, theologians, and pastors, ignore the many passages in Scripture where God is described as displaying certain emotions. Emotions are divine, but we have an irrational fear of an emotional God.

WHY DON'T WE WANT TO ASSOCIATE EMOTIONS WITH GOD?

When it comes to God and emotions, we have two problems. First, certain emotions are commonly viewed negatively, such as hate, anger, and jealousy, which are particularly problematic to associate with God—and yet the Bible frequently does just that. These negative emotions don't fit with how we think God should act. There is a tension between the textual portrayal of God and what we "know" to be true of God. How are we to understand a God who hates, gets angry, and is jealous?

Second, emotions are often perceived to be irrational, uncontrollable, and confusing. We don't want to associate them with God ("no crying he makes"). We feel more comfortable with a God who is rational, predicable, and comprehensible, so biblical texts that describe God with human emotions are often discounted. We do this to protect God's honor, but since the God we find in the Bible is in fact highly emotional, our de-emphasizing his divine emotions doesn't honor him—it distorts his character. As we will see from the psalms and elsewhere, the emotional side of God is not to be hidden but praised.

Let's examine some of the ways emotions are viewed negatively. While there are negative emotions (e.g., hate, anger, jealousy), many emotions are generally perceived positively (e.g., love, compassion, joy). Despite the perception of these positive emotions, there is still a negative bias against emotional behavior in general. There are at least three factors that contribute to this negative perspective on emotions.

Emotions seem irrational. Emotions cloud our ability to think reasonably, and in our enlightened world where rationality is king, anything that inhibits reason is bad. Sir Arthur Conan Doyle gives voice to this perspective from the mouth of his famous detective, as Sherlock Holmes says to John Watson, "The emotional qualities are antagonistic to clear reasoning."[3] Fortunately, Holmes's brain was never encumbered by emotions.

Because we think of God as purely rational, and not controlled by emotions, when his emotions affect him, it doesn't make sense. When God saw the wickedness of the humans he had created, before he told Noah to build an ark, the text says God regretted making the humans (Gen 6:6). Why would an omniscient God regret creating humankind when he knew what they were like and what they would do? It seems irrational. Apparently, God needs to learn to control his emotions, which leads to the next problem.

Emotions seem uncontrollable. Emotions can be so difficult to control, so unpredictable; they become dangerous. Emotions can prompt us to do stupid things we later regret. In the film *Captain Marvel* (2019), Yon-Rogg (Jude Law) repeatedly warns Vers (Captain Marvel, played by Brie Larson) about how she needs to control her emotions, "There's nothing more dangerous to a warrior than emotion."

When we read the story of Uzzah and the ark (2 Sam 6:1-11), we wonder why God chose to smite poor Uzzah in anger when he was trying only to help by preventing the ark from tipping over. On an initial reading of this story, it seems like God can't control his anger.[4] For people who grew up with angry, abusive parents, the biblical portrayal of an angry God could trigger traumatic memories. They experienced plenty of uncontrollable emotions when they were young. They want nothing to do with an unpredictable God of wrath.

Emotions seem confusing. We don't understand emotions. Some of us don't even know what emotion we are feeling. We're just upset. Why do these types of situations make me feel so uncomfortable?

When I was fourteen, I vividly remember the first of several times that I was dumped by a girlfriend. (One reason I remember it so clearly is that deep emotions make deep impressions on our memories.) I went out to the woods to be by myself. I sat down on a tree stump and cried. I was hurt, but what made it even more difficult was that I didn't know what to do, what to say, or who to talk to. What was I feeling? I just felt bad. I'd never felt like that before. I told no one because I was confused.

Emotions are confusing, particularly when it comes to God. Why does a God of love hate people (Mal 2:3)? Why does God say he is jealous (Ex 34:14)—isn't he fully content just being God? What does it mean for God that he delights or rejoices over his people (Is 62:4)? We want God to be predictable, but the God of the Bible is mysterious, sometimes confusing, and often emotional.

Is God impassible? Because emotions are generally perceived to be irrational, uncontrollable, and confusing—we don't want to associate them with God. The theological rationale for denying God is emotional is based on the idea of divine impassibility, the view that God is unaffected emotionally by human behavior. Instead of speaking of emotions, scholars sometimes speak of God's passions. Even though the issue of divine impassibility is relevant to this discussion of God's emotions, I will not discuss it in depth. Discussions of the topic quickly become highly theological, philosophical, and abstract, which may be fascinating to theologians and Bible scholars, but not so much to folks who don't read Hebrew, Greek, or Latin.[5] While many people I respect affirm it, divine impassibility is not a doctrine I subscribe to because of the overwhelming amount of biblical evidence—as we will see in this book—which describes the God of both testaments as affected emotionally by the behavior of humans.[6]

"Feelings are your enemy." We find a negative perspective on emotions in many other contexts. Old Testament professor Jack Deere writes about his experience in theological education, "In one of my

first classes, a professor said to us, 'Liberals feel; we think.' The students roared. The message was clear, *Feelings are your enemy. They cloud your mind and endanger your faith.* I embraced that message."[7] Deere's story feels hyperbolic, but after living in the world of theological higher education for twenty-five years, I can relate. While it is perhaps less so now than in the past, traditionally, emotions have been viewed as an enemy.

When theological professors perceive emotions negatively, they won't connect them with God. Biblical texts that portray God emotionally will be ignored, de-emphasized, or discounted. Professors won't teach about divine emotions to seminary students. This legacy of not teaching texts that don't fit a certain theology will then be passed on to the next generations of professors, pastors, and Sunday school teachers. As a result, the folks in the pew rarely hear about the anger, the sorrow, or the joy of God.

A STORY, OR A DRAMA, BUT NOT A SONG

A subtle way emotions are de-emphasized in the teaching of the church is by highlighting prose narratives and ignoring poetry. Typically, the psalms and prophetic poetry of the Old Testament have higher concentrations of emotive language than prose narratives. When the Bible is summarized in books or churches, the narratives are emphasized, and the poetry is often ignored. The Bible is summarized as a story, or a drama, but not a song.[8] The makers of *Brian's Song* realized there is emotive power in characterizing Piccolo's life as a song.

When children are taught in Sunday school they learn about the heroes of the Old Testament: Abraham, Moses, Gideon, Ruth, David, and Esther. But children rarely learn about heroic prophets such as Isaiah, Jeremiah, Ezekiel, Hosea, Habakkuk, and Haggai, who speak for God in poetry. Over the course of almost six decades of listening to sermons, I've heard far more coming out of narrative texts than poetic or prophetic texts. I've certainly preached more sermons from narrative than poetry.

In this book, we'll be discussing texts throughout the Bible, but much of the time we'll be looking at poetic books to understand how and why God expresses emotions. For example, God's emotions come to the fore clearly in the book of Hosea. Here is what I say elsewhere about Hosea, "The emotive poetry depicting God's heartbreak over the trauma of his broken relationship with his people is unmatched anywhere else in Scripture."[9] Castelo lists God's emotional expressions in Hosea, "God's indecisiveness (Hos 6:4; 11:8), anger (Hos 8:5; 13:11; 14:4 [14:5]), hatred (Hos 9:15), love (Hos 11:1; 14:4 [14:5]), compassion (Hos 11:8), and wrath (Hos 13:11)."[10] Brueggemann states, "The plenitude of images (in Hosea) is daring, offensive and evocative. . . . Hosea dares to take us inside that complex interior life of Yahweh and thus to be exposed to a range of divine impulses not elsewhere available in Israel's ancient text."[11] I confess I have spent little time reading, studying, or teaching the emotionally rich book of Hosea. I suspect that I'm not unique in this regard.

Poetry is where divine emotions are expressed most vividly and dramatically. By ignoring poetic texts, pastors, teachers, and seminary professors are, to use the language of Paul (2 Tim 3:16), depriving their audiences of learning—of profiting—from all inspired Scripture about the emotions of God and God's people.

THE FRUIT OF THE SPIRIT AND WORKS OF THE FLESH

A variety of emotions appear in Paul's list of the fruit of the Spirit and the works of the flesh (Gal 5:16-26). Paul lists nine fruit of the Spirit and fifteen works of the flesh, many of which would be described as behaviors not emotions (e.g., drunkenness, self-control). Here I'll only mention the ones that are more emotional in nature.

Positive emotions are fruit of the Spirit (Gal 5:22-23) and are often associated with God, for example: "joy" (*chara*), "kindness" (*chrēstotēs*), and "love" (*agapē*). Ideally, followers of Jesus will be guided by the Spirit into manifesting these fruits in our lives.

Paul contrasts these spiritual fruits, with fleshly works. Several emotions commonly perceived negatively are works not of the Spirit but of the flesh (Gal 5:19-21). Despite their fleshly nature, three of these works of the flesh are surprisingly associated with God: "hatred" (*echthra*), "anger" (*thymos*), and "jealousy" (*zēlos*). Paul warns us against these works—but what about when God hates, is angry, or is jealous? What are we to do with that?

To summarize, when it comes to God and emotions, we have two problems. First, because emotions seem irrational, uncontrollable, and confusing, we don't want to associate them with God. Second, negatively perceived emotions like hate, anger, and jealousy are works of the flesh, but the Bible connects them to God. So far, we've looked at the downside of emotions and an emotional God. The rest of this chapter will focus more on the upside of emotions, and why it is good that our God is an emotional God, but first we need to define emotions.

WHAT ARE EMOTIONS?

What are emotions? While we all have them, and we generally know what they are, emotions are still difficult to define.[12] In the appendix to his book, *Emotional Intelligence*, titled, "What Is Emotion?" Daniel Coleman observes that psychologists and philosophers have "quibbled" over the meaning of emotions for "more than a century."[13]

Emotions are feelings, particularly strong ones, that are prompted by circumstances, moods, and relationships.[14] They're distinct from reasoning and knowledge. While theologians use the word *passion* for emotion, outside theological circles, passion often connotes strong, or barely controllable emotions. These definitions provide a

good starting point, but as is often the case, it's a bit more complicated, particularly as we observe how emotions are expressed
in Scripture.

Emotions involve actions. Neuroscientists, psychologists, and philosophers define emotions differently because of the distinct nature
of their disciplines. Likewise, we will reflect here on how emotion is
understood biblically. For example, in the Bible, emotions are often
inextricably tied to actions and behaviors. They aren't pure feelings
in one's head or heart. We see several examples of this linkage in
Jesus' Sermon on the Mount. Jesus equates being angry with a
brother to insulting a brother, and these behaviors are comparable
to murder in that they are both liable to similar punishments
(Mt 5:21-22). For Jesus, there isn't a clear distinction between feeling
angry and acting on that feeling to harm others. A few verses later
(Mt 5:43-47), Jesus takes a familiar saying, "love your neighbor and
hate your enemy," and gives it a shocking twist. Jesus tells them to
love their enemies, which doesn't just involve warm feelings, but
concrete actions like praying for enemies and greeting strangers. A
few verses after that (Mt 6:24), Jesus speaks of hate and love in the
context of service to a master. If one has two masters, only one will
be served and loved, the other will be despised and hated. Once
again, the emotions of love and hate manifest themselves in tangible
behaviors, in this case intense loyalty and disloyalty.

Jesus concludes the Beatitudes with a command to rejoice and be
glad (Mt 5:12). Throughout the Gospels, feelings of joy are connected to rejoicing and praising (Lk 6:23; 10:20; 15:6, 9; Jn 3:29;
16:22). In his *Reflections on the Psalms*, C. S. Lewis explains this
linkage, "We delight to praise what we enjoy because the praise not
merely expresses but completes the enjoyment . . . the delight is
incomplete till it is expressed."[15] Early in the Covid-19 pandemic,
churches were prohibited from meeting, which meant believers were
unable to gather to sing and praise. It was painful to lay down our

delight in corporate worship of God, but we did it to love our neighbors and keep them safe.

We don't need to move outside the Gospels, to find other examples of emotions connected with actions. When Jesus saw a leper, he didn't just feel compassion, but it moved him to heal the man (Mk 1:41). When Jesus saw Mary weeping over her brother Lazarus's death, his compassion and grief prompted him to weep, which in turn led those watching to comment, "See how he loved him!" (Jn 11:32-36). In Scripture, emotions are felt, acted on, and witnessed.

Emotions can be rational. At this point, let's revisit and revise the three negative statements that were made earlier about emotions. First, emotions can be rational. In *Emotional Intelligence*, Daniel Coleman cites research from neurologist Antonio Damasio who concludes, counterintuitively "that feelings are typically indispensable for rational decisions; they point us in the proper direction, where dry logic can then be of best use."[16] It is rational to feel fear when facing a severe threat like a wild animal. While camping on our honeymoon at Tuolumne Meadows at Yosemite Park, there was a bear rummaging around outside our tent. It would have been irrational to not feel fear in that context. Screaming in panic would have been irrational and counterproductive, but alertness and caution prompted by fear could have saved our lives. (However, while scuba diving in Florida, I once spotted a shark, but I wasn't afraid—all my diving buddies were between me and the shark. They would have made a tastier snack than me.) It is totally rational to feel love for my spouse of thirty years, and I certainly hope it isn't irrational for her to love me too. It makes sense to love spouses. I dare you to tell a friend, "It's irrational for your wife to love you." Let me know what he says. Emotions aren't purely rational, but neither are they purely irrational.

Emotions can be controlled. Second, emotions can be controlled. It isn't always easy, but it's not impossible. God commands his people to love him (Deut 6:5; 11:1; Josh 22:5), to fear him (Lev 19:14, 32; 25:17), to delight in him (Is 58:14), to rejoice in him (Ps 97:12; Is 41:16; Joel 2:23). If emotions can be commanded, they can be controlled. We are commanded to "be angry, and do not sin" (Ps 4:4; Eph 4:26). Not only is God described as being slow to anger (Ex 34:6; Jon 4:2), but God's Word encourages his people to be slow to anger (Prov 14:29; Jas 1:19). Even anger can be controlled. The fact that emotions are commanded and controlled suggests conscious reasoning affects our manifestations of them. I have a health app on my phone, which gives a small challenge each day to earn points. As I wrote this, the challenge for today was "Pause . . . when difficulties arise, it's easy to let emotions control your actions. But if you pause to check in with yourself first, you're more likely to respond thoughtfully rather than react emotionally." Health apps think emotions can be controlled. But our control of emotions should not be misconstrued to become emotional suppression. Emotions are meant to be embraced. God commands love, fear, delight, and rejoicing because they are healthy expressions of our relationship with him.

Emotions can be understood. Third, emotions can be understood. They are often confusing and mysterious, but this doesn't mean they are incomprehensible. Reflecting on how emotions can be rational and controllable helps us understand them. As we examine the many places that Scripture mentions emotions, we gain greater understanding about how not only to control them, but to express them, and to use them to bless others. As any of us who speak regularly with a close friend, a counselor, or a spiritual director knows, talking about emotions brings clarity.

THE SEVEN EMOTIONS OF GOD

The Emotions of God will look at the seven emotions that are most frequently associated with God in the Bible. We will begin with three negatively perceived ("bad") divine emotions: hate (chap. 2), anger (chap. 3), and jealousy (chap. 4). The middle chapter is a bridge chapter focused on sorrow (chap. 5). We will conclude with three positively perceived ("good") divine emotions: joy (chap. 6), compassion (chap. 7), and love (chap. 8).

If we examine other classic discussions of emotions, we find these seven emotions, as well as a few others.[17] I'll briefly mention four standard lists (see table 1.1). Aristotle discusses the role emotions play in public speech in his classic work *Rhetoric* and lists ten basic emotions: enmity, anger, indignation, envy, kindness, pity, love, fear, shame, and friendship—seven of which are roughly comparable to five of mine.[18] In *The Expressions of the Emotions on Man and Animals*, Charles Darwin examines how emotional expressions affect biological behavior. Darwin's list includes a wider variety of emotions than Aristotle (e.g., hatred, contempt, disgust, weeping, joy, tender feelings, love, fear, surprise, and shame), with parallels for all but one of the emotions discussed here (jealousy).[19] The psychologist Robert Plutchik visualized distinct types of emotions in a wheel: disgust, anger, sadness, joy, love, fear, surprise, and trust.[20]

Plutchik's wheel includes eight "spokes," with three levels of increasing intensity as one moves toward the center (for example, 1. annoyance, 2. anger, 3. rage), plus eight other bridge emotions hovering on the outside between each of these spokes—thus his model includes thirty-two emotional descriptors (love is one of his outer bridge emotions, so my table includes nine for him). His model includes equivalents for five of my seven (all except jealousy and compassion). The final classic list of emotions, and the shortest, is found in the 2015 Pixar film *Inside Out*.[21] The five emotions of *Inside Out* are disgust, anger, sadness, joy, and fear, each of which are personified in the mind of the main character, a young girl named Riley.

While there is variety among these four lists of emotions, all of the emotions focused on in this book appear in some form in at least

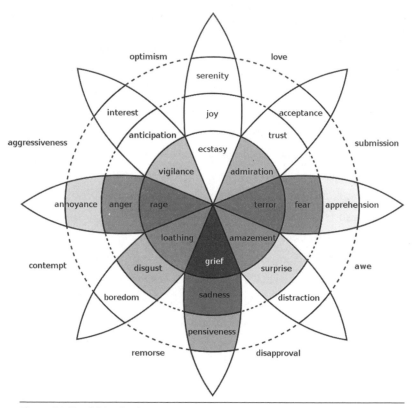

Figure 1.1. Plutchik's wheel

one list, and all except one (jealousy) are included in most of these lists. There are differences in terminology between my lists and these other four, but the basic emotion described is comparable. My terms are based on words found in standard English Bible translations. Hate is not identical to enmity (Aristotle), contempt, or disgust (Darwin, Plutchik, *Inside Out*), but they are all roughly synonymous, likewise for sorrow, weeping, and sadness. Three of the emotions that appear on several of these other lists—fear, shame, and surprise—are not attributed to God in the Bible and therefore won't be discussed.

Each chapter of this book will focus on one of these emotions. The chapter will define it, examine words the Bible uses for it, look

Table 1.1. Emotions in the Bible, Aristotle, Darwin, Plutchik, and *Inside Out*

Chapter Discussed	Biblical term	Aristotle	Darwin	Plutchik	*Inside Out*
2	Hate	Enmity	Hatred, contempt, disgust	Disgust	Disgust
3	Anger	Anger and indignation	Anger	Anger	Anger
4	Jealousy	Envy			
5	Sorrow		Weeping	Sadness	Sadness
6	Joy		Joy	Joy	Joy
7	Compassion	Kindness and pity	Tender feelings		
8	Love	Love	Love	Love	
Not "Divine"		Fear, shame, friendship	Fear, surprise, shame	Fear, surprise, trust, anticipation	Fear

at how God displays it, and then discuss how we can follow God's example of expressing emotions in a way that blesses others. As we search the Scriptures to see where God is behaving emotionally, we discover a variety of synonyms used by English translations for a specific divine emotion. For example, passages that speak of God's wrath (Jn 3:36), his fury (Rev 19:15), or his indignation (Ps 102:10) are all related to his anger, and therefore could be discussed in the anger chapter.

At this point, we need to make a comment about the prioritization of these emotions, lest one think that all seven are equally attributed to God. Two of these emotions are connected to God in the Bible far less frequently than the others: hatred and jealousy. And three of them are associated with God more frequently: wrath, compassion and love. If there were "one emotion to rule them all," it would clearly be love, since all of these emotions are somehow manifestations of God's loving character. John captures this truth well in his refrain, "God is love" (1 Jn 4:8, 16).

THE EMOTIONS OF THE PSALMS

While the book of Psalms is often skipped over when the Bible is summarized as a story, it has always been popular. One of the many reasons people love the psalms is they are filled with beautiful and intense emotional language, as the psalmist expresses passion for God, hate toward enemies, and joy over God's Word. The Psalms therefore serve as a good introduction to divine emotions.

The Psalms are quoted or alluded to in the New Testament more than any other Old Testament book.[22] While many factors contribute to this phenomenon, one reason for their popularity is their rich emotional language. In the prayers of the psalmist, God is frequently described emotionally, and all seven divine emotions examined here are mentioned in the psalms.

God hates (Ps 5:5; 11:5; 45:7).

God gets angry (Ps 6:1; 30:5; 78:21).

God is jealous (Ps 78:58; 79:5).

God is grieved (Ps 78:40).

God delights (Ps 18:20; 22:8; 35:27).

God shows mercy (Ps 25:6; 28:6; 103:4).

God loves (Ps 5:7; 25:6; 136).

According to the Psalms, emotions are divine.

This deeply emotive book teaches the people of God how to praise. Interestingly, the title of the book in Hebrew, *Tehillim*, means "Praises." The book of Psalms reveals that God's emotions are not to be ignored or hidden, but they are to be praised, sung, and shouted to the nations.

At this point, I should make a comment about names for God.[23] The name God is called by far the most in the Bible is Yahweh (over 6,800 times). All of these are located in the Old Testament, and most English translations render his name as "the LORD." Psalm 69 calls him "Yahweh" five times (vv. 6, 13, 16, 31, 33). Though Jesus is called many names in the New Testament (Son of Man,

Christ), the name he is called most frequently is simply "Jesus." While discussing passages, I will generally follow the text, so I'll often speak of Yahweh in the Old Testament and Jesus in the New. Names are important.

THE EMOTIONS OF PSALM 69

While the psalms generally use rich, emotive language, there are a few psalms that stand out as particularly emotive, like Psalm 69. It is full of emotional language, mentioning all seven of the emotions that we will focus on in this book. The subjects of these emotional expressions include the psalmist (zeal, v. 9; sorrow, v. 10), the psalmist's enemies (hate, v. 4), and people blessed by God (gladness, v. 32; love, v. 36).

But the person described with the most emotions in this psalm is God (emphasis added):

> But I pray to you, LORD,
>   in the time of your favor;
> in your great **love** (*hesed*), O God,
>   answer me with your sure salvation . . .
> Answer me, LORD, out of the goodness of your **love** (*hesed*);
> in your great **mercy** (*rahamim*) turn to me. (Ps 69:13, 16)

In a desperate cry for salvation, the psalmist appeals to God's love (vv. 13, 16) and to God's mercy (v. 16).

> This will **please** (*yatav*) the LORD more than an ox,
>   more than a bull with its horns and hooves . . .

Yahweh will be pleased with praise and thanksgiving more than an ox (v. 31; I wouldn't think the ox cares).

Perhaps the most powerful expression of divine emotions in Psalm 69 comes in the middle of a prayer of cursing in verses 22-28 (emphasis added).

May the table set before them become a snare;
    may it become retribution and a trap.
May their eyes be darkened so they cannot see,
    and their backs be bent forever.
Pour out your **wrath** (*za'am*) on them;
    let your **fierce anger** (*haron 'ap*) overtake them.
May their place be deserted;
    let there be no one to dwell in their tents.
For they persecute those you wound
    and talk about the pain of those you hurt.
Charge them with crime upon crime;
    do not let them share in your salvation.
May they be blotted out of the book of life
and not be listed with the righteous. (Ps 69:22-28)

Because of all the hate, scorn, and shame from his enemies, the psalmist prays for God's wrath to be poured out upon them and for his fierce anger to overtake them (v. 24). While the psalmist never explicitly uses the word hate here, the tone in this imprecatory prayer sounds hateful. The psalmist wants them to be trapped, darkened, bent over, deserted, indicted for crimes, and most dramatically, deleted from God's book of life.

While one might think Psalm 69 isn't merely describing the emotional life of God, but merely what the psalmist believes he is feeling, the fact that this psalm is included in the Word of God and is therefore divinely inspired means that God has authorized its usage for our lives of faith. So, what do we do with psalms like this that include curses? We will discuss the hate and anger of imprecatory prayers like Psalm 69 in chapters two and three, but at this point we can state that intense emotions are disturbing and sometimes they just need to be expressed. From Psalm 69, we can make three points about prayer and emotions.

First, the psalmist prays emotionally. This psalm contains a lot of rich, emotional language (hate, love, zeal, weeping, scorn, hope, mercy, wrath, anger, gladness, and pleasure). Most of these emotions are repeated within the psalm. It is hard to find a verse in Psalm 69 that does not include a deep expression of emotion. Notice also the first emotion mentioned here is hate, and the final one mentioned is love, thus we see a movement from hate to love, reminiscent of Jesus (Mt 5:43-44). Psalms are not only prayers, but they are included in Scripture to model for believers how to pray. If we are to pray like the psalmist, we will pray emotionally.

Second, the psalmist prays hyperbolically. The emotions expressed here by the psalmist are extreme. The psalmist is drowning (vv. 1-2, 14-15), has failing voice and eyes (v. 3), has more enemies than hair (v. 4; if bald, it's not too bad), is abandoned by family (v. 8), is taunted by all, including drunkards (7, 9-12). We don't know exactly what is happening to the psalmist here, but the tone is hyperbolic.[24] The psalmist may have been tossed into the sea like Jonah (Jon 1:15), but it is far more likely that the experience makes the psalmist feel like they are drowning. The extremity of the language is necessary to effectively communicate the intensity of the feelings of hate, abandonment, and shame. The hyperbolic language gives honest expression to the severe nature of their experience. The psalmist needed to vent. Is it totally rational? No, but it is biblical. If we make rationality our primary goal in prayer, it would preclude utilizing the Psalms. The Psalms help us connect our emotional selves to our emotional God.

When I teach a course on the Psalms, I assign students to write a psalm of lament, like Psalm 69. Not surprisingly, many students find it difficult to be raw, honest, or extreme in their laments. One of the most frequent comments I make on their papers is "Use hyperbole like the psalms." Instead of "I feel sad" say, "I'm devastated . . . I'm drowning . . . I have come into the deep waters, the floods engulf me." If we are to pray like the psalmist, we will pray hyperbolically.

Third, the psalmist prays to an emotional God. The author of
Psalm 69 has no qualms about expressing emotions hyperbolically
and appealing to a highly emotional God. The God the psalmist
describes shows mercy, loves, is pleased, and pours out fierce anger
and wrath. While we may feel uncomfortable with emotions, or particularly an emotional God, the New Testament authors connect this
highly emotional psalm frequently to Jesus.

There are perhaps only two psalms referenced in the New Testament more often than Psalm 69, which is referenced at least
thirteen times:[25] *Hated without reason* (v. 4) is quoted by Jesus in
reference to the world's hatred of him (Jn 15:25). *Zeal for God's house*
(v. 9a) is recalled by Jesus' disciples after he cleanses the temple
(Jn 2:17). *Insults have fallen on me* (v. 9b) is quoted by Paul as he
argues how Jesus did not please himself (Rom 15:3). *Given vinegar
for my thirst* (v. 21) is alluded to in all four of the Gospels when Jesus
is offered a drink while on the cross (Mt 27:34, 48; Mk 15:23, 36;
Lk 23:36; Jn 19:28-30). *The table as a trap . . . their backs bent* (vv. 22-23)
is quoted by Paul in describing God's attitude toward his own people
Israel, a temporary rejection (Rom 11:9-10). *Place be deserted* (v. 25a)
is alluded to by Jesus as he laments over Jerusalem (Mt 23:38), and
let no one dwell (v. 25) is quoted in Acts in connection to the selection
of Matthias to replace Judas (Acts 1:20).

While we may feel uncomfortable with an emotional God, or with
a person praying in an emotional, hyperbolic, almost hateful manner,
New Testament authors have no such qualms. Not only do they quote
this psalm, but they repeatedly connect it to Jesus. James Mays calls this,
"A passion psalm of Christ."[26] In his comments on Psalm 69, John
Goldingay states, "There is some irony in the fact that the point where
the NT (New Testament) concentrates most of its use of the psalm is
where commentators see it as unworthy of the NT."[27] If we are to pray
like the psalmist, we will pray to an emotional God. As we broaden our

focus beyond the Psalms, we will discover that all of Scripture uses emotional language to describe God. It's not just the Psalms.

INSIDE OUT

Shortly after it came out my family saw the Pixar film *Inside Out* (2015) in the theater (spoiler warning). The film powerfully reveals how each of our emotions plays an important role in the life and welfare of a person. The story focuses on a young girl named Riley who makes a traumatic move with her family from Minnesota to San Francisco.

Much of the story is set inside Riley's head as she experiences strong emotions resulting from the move. In case you've forgotten from a few pages ago, the emotional personifications are Joy, Sadness, Anger, Fear, and Disgust. Joy runs the show inside Riley's emotional Headquarters, but gets literally sucked into Riley's memory, along with Sadness, where she is stranded. Riley's previously well-ordered world devolves with Anger, Fear, and Disgust in control. In her tumultuous journey back to Headquarters, Joy encounters Bing Bong, Riley's imaginary friend, who looks like the strange love child of Barney and a Heffalump. (If you don't know who these two creatures are, it's too hard to explain; just google them.)

Bing Bong struggles to help Joy escape from the Memory Dump as they ride his wagon-rocket. But each attempt fails because they're too heavy. Right before one last wagon ride, Bing Bong assures Joy that this time she will be successful. As they are rocketing up, Bing Bong intentionally lets go. The loss of his "ballast" allows Joy to rocket up with the necessary speed to escape the Memory Dump. As he falls backward, Bing Bong fades away. At this point my whole family is convulsing with tears (uncontrollable sobbing makes covert weeping difficult).

Why was that scene so powerful? It was a combination of emotions. The fear of abandonment. The joy of escape. The love of a friend. But perhaps the most powerful emotion here was the sadness of loss. We grieve over the sacrifice, motivated by the love of an imaginary friend who allowed himself to be destined to oblivion for the sake of Joy, for the sake of Riley. There's power in sacrificial love.

While it looks different, Scripture makes a similar point. The Bible speaks of a tapestry of emotions, rich and beautiful, that are felt not only by humans, but also by God. These emotions add flavor, color, and depth to our lives. When we minimize, dismiss, or discount the emotions of God in Scripture, we shortchange ourselves. We don't fully profit (to use Paul's language in 2 Timothy 3:16) from what God is saying to us through his Word.

Perhaps the clearest example of this is Jesus' death. Often the cross is spoken about primarily in a transactional way (particularly in the West) as we emphasize, often quite dispassionately, the price Jesus paid for our sins. While this perspective is certainly valid, there is more to the story. Scripture also describes Jesus' death emotionally. There is a reason it is called the passion of the Christ.

It's been a long time since I cried at Easter. But there's power in sacrificial love. We should all grieve every year over the sacrifice, motivated by the love of a true friend, who allowed himself to be crucified for the sake of the world. As we examine the emotions of God in each chapter, we'll keep revisiting the passion of the Christ.

2

the hatred of god

I have loved Jacob, but Esau I have hated.

MALACHI 1:2-3

"WHY DO THEY HATE US SO MUCH? ... Women and Jews—
what threat do we pose to those men, that they call for our deaths?"
In the historical novel *Resistance Women* (2019), two Jewish sisters,
Amalie and Sara, have just witnessed rioting in the streets of Berlin,
which prompts Amalie to lament with these questions to her family
about Nazi hatred of Jews.[1] This interaction is set in October 1930,
when the Nazis were violently celebrating recent political success,
rising from a small minority to become the second most powerful
party in the German parliament. Rioters were chanting in the streets
of Berlin, "Heil Hitler! Germany Awake! Death to the Jews!"[2]

While the past century has known many groups associated with
hate—Boko Haram, the Ku Klux Klan, al-Qaeda—none have slaughtered as many innocent objects of their hatred as the Nazis. Their
hideous actions began long before WWII. The Nazi slogan "Death to
the Jews" was popularized more than a decade before the systematic
killings began. Yet tragically the world, and even the church in Germany,
stood by and did nothing to stop their barbaric crimes fueled by hatred
despite the obvious signs. It should have been no surprise that the

Nazis delivered on their promise of "Death to the Jews!" as they attempted genocide by murdering over six million Jews.

We are justifiably troubled by the hatred of people toward other people. People who hate others, like the Nazis, are evil. But what about a God who hates?

Problematically, God is repeatedly described as hating not only certain behaviors, but also many people. One of the most disturbing examples of this problematic divine behavior is found in the book of Malachi, "I have loved Jacob, but Esau I have hated" (Mal 1:2-3). Why does God hate Esau, but love Jacob? How can we make sense of a God who hates? Before we address these questions, we need to define hate.

DEFINING HATE

The word *hate* can mean something we don't like doing. If I were to say to you, "I hate to bother you . . . ," you should expect an attempt to be bothered, suggesting that this particular manifestation of hatred isn't sufficient to quash said annoyance. If you told a friend, "I hate to fly," they would understand that you have a strong aversion toward air travel, and they might reply, "Me too!" You may proceed to talk together about all those minor inconveniences you encountered over the many, many times you chose to do this very thing you "hate." People who speak of hating in these contexts would not be described as hateful people. It is good to dislike bothering others, and it is reasonable to dislike flying in planes. However, in both cases these supposed hatreds are easily overcome since interruptions and crowded airplanes are frequent phenomena. We use the term *hate* hyperbolically for dramatic effect when we are speaking about things we don't enjoy or we find uncomfortable.

When the Bible speaks of hatred, sometimes hyperbolically, the word isn't merely associated with discomfort. In Scripture, *hate* means to feel strong dislike or disgust toward something. Synonyms include *loathe, detest, abhor,* or *despise.* In Plutchik's wheel of emotions, the closest equivalent emotional "spoke" to hatred begins with boredom, intensifying to disgust, then finally loathing.

Many people in Scripture hate things and people, which isn't surprising. What is surprising—and troubling—is that God is often described as hating things and people.

WORDS OF HATRED

Unlike some of the other divine emotions, the Bible doesn't use a lot of words for hate. In table 2.1, I've included words used in both the Old and New Testament for *hatred* (the first two words are Hebrew, the third is Greek).

Table 2.1. Hate in the Old and New Testament

Hebrew/ Greek	English	Divine anger examples (ESV) (emphasis added)	Other references
sana'	hate	I **hate**, I despise your religious festivals; your assemblies are a stench to me (Amos 5:21).	Ps 5:6; 11:5; Is 1:14; Jer 12:8; Hos 9:15
sin'ah	hatred	And you murmured in your tents and said, "Because the Lord **hated** us he has brought us out of the land of Egypt" (Deut 1:27).	Deut 9:28
miseō	hate	If anyone comes to me and does not **hate** his own father and mother and wife and children and brothers and sisters, yes, and even his own life, he cannot be my disciple (Lk 14:26).	

In the Old Testament, the primary Hebrew word for hate is the verb *sana'*, "hate" (Prov 6:16), which appears 148 times. It is primarily used in reference to human hatred of other humans (Gen 37:4, 5, 8), but it is also used of God's hatred both of actions (Amos 5:21) and people (Jer 12:8). The related noun *sin'ah*, "hatred," is also used primarily for human hatred (Ps 139:22). It is used twice for God (Deut 1:27; 9:28), but in both of these texts people who are opposed to God are accusing him of hating (*sin'ah*) his people. The Greek verb for *hate* in the New Testament is the verb *miseō* which appears forty times, usually of people toward others (Lk 1:71; 6:27). It is used perhaps most provocatively by Jesus as he commands his followers to essentially hate their family (Lk 14:26).

HOW CAN A GOD OF LOVE ALSO BE A GOD OF HATE?

The God of the Bible is an emotional God, but there are certain emotions that we more naturally associate with him than others. We like a God who expresses positive emotions like love and compassion, particularly when we are the recipients. But a God who expresses negative emotions like hate and anger is disturbing, particularly when we are the targets.

Hatred is one of the works of the flesh (Gal 5:20), which are contrasted with the fruit of the spirit, the first of which is love (Gal 5:22). Love comes from the divine spirit, and hate comes from human flesh. Love is the ideal emotion, what we should strive for in all our relationships. Hatred is the opposite of love. The people we associate with hate are White supremacists, the Taliban, and Nazis.

There are few things more troubling in Scripture than the hatred of God. One of the most common refrains spoken about God is that he is love (1 Jn 4:8, 16).

How can a God of love also be a God of hate?

"A TIME TO HATE . . ."

The author of Ecclesiastes doesn't provide a clear rationale for divine hatred but suggests that hate has a place in the divinely inspired order of the universe. In the paradoxical "a time for everything" poem of Ecclesiastes 3, the author states,

> There is a time for everything . . .
> a time to love, and a time to hate (*sana'*),
> a time for war and a time for peace. (Eccles 3:1, 8)

Love and hate are given their appropriate time along with other things including birth and death (v. 1), killing and healing (v. 3), weeping and laughing (v. 4), and war and peace (v. 8). We love birth, healing, laughing, and peace. And yet each of their negative counterparts (death, killing, weeping, and war) has their time appointed, presumably, by God. This poem may not make it clear, but the rest of the book of Ecclesiastes clarifies that God is sovereign in our lives to bring both good and bad (Eccles 1:13; 2:24; 3:10; 5:18; 6:2; 7:14; 8:15; 9:7). According to the Word of God, there is a time to hate. When is that time?

GOD HATES EVIL

Most of the texts that speak about divine hatred do so in the context of his response to sin. God hates pride (Ps 5:5), divorce (Mal 2:16), robbery, wrong (Is 61:8), violence, bloodshed (Ps 11:5; Ezek 35:6), evil, and wickedness (Ps 5:5; 11:5; 45:7; Amos 5:15). While all of these things are reasonable targets for hatred, the text still provides an explanation for why God hates them. He hates evil because he loves justice (Is 61:8; Amos 5:15), because he loves good (Amos 5:15), and because he loves righteousness (Ps 45:7). God's hatred of these things is part of what makes him good.

Any of us who have been robbed, attacked, or victimized can relate. In 1994, I was leading a missions trip to a country in central Asia. While I was riding a bus, $2,400 and ten passports were stolen out of my backpack by a thief. I was devastated, and angry at God for allowing this to happen while we were doing his work. God eventually provided for us miraculously in response to our desperate prayers, but I had never hated robbery more in my life.

The intensity of my hatred was directly proportional to how negatively this theft affected me personally. I am not typically bothered when other people are robbed or victims of violence, unless they are close to me. However, God hates all evil actions (robbery, violence, or bloodshed) even when he isn't the primary victim. Why? Because these acts of evil negatively affect what he cares deeply about: humans, created in his image (Gen 1:26-27).

GOD'S LEAST FAVORITE THINGS

The book of Proverbs lists objects of divine hatred. These are a few of God's least favorite things.

> There are six things the LORD hates (*sana'*)
> seven that are detestable (*to'evah*) to him:
> haughty eye,
> a lying tongue,
> hands that shed innocent blood,
> a heart that devises wicked schemes,
> feet that are quick to rush into evil,
> a false witness who pours out lies,
> and a person who stirs up conflict in the community.
>   (Prov 6:16-19)

While it may seem a bit confusing (does God hate six or seven things?), this type of numerical pattern (x, followed by x + 1) is a common device in biblical poetry (see Prov 30:15, 18, 21, 29; Amos 1:3, 6, 9, 11, 13; 2:1, 4, 6). Kidner thinks it is a way of showing the list is specific, but not exhaustive.[3]

Interestingly, the objects of God's hatred in Proverbs 6 are body parts. The detestable list includes five organs, starting at the top (eyes and tongue, v. 17), moving to the middle (hands and heart, vv. 17c-18a), and ending at the bottom (feet, v. 18b). As it concludes, the poem broadens from specific parts, to witness (v. 19a) which involves multiple organs (tongue, mouth, heart, and mind) and then to a whole person (v. 19b). Why is God picking on these parts? Because they are causing harm.

Our bodies' each and every part is good. God created all of them (Gen 1:26-31). When our body parts are functioning as they were designed, they would not provoke divine hatred. The text therefore adds a description to each explaining why God finds them detestable in this context. The sins here that God hates overlap with the evil actions that were mentioned in the previous section: pride (haughty eyes), deception (lying tongue, false witness, lies), violence (bloody hands), and evil more generally (wicked schemes, evil feet). The list culminates with people who are stirring up conflict in the community. When these sins come together the result is a breakdown in fellowship, thus prompting the divine hatred.

Pride lifts people up while putting others down. Deception cheats, robs, and damages others. Violence causes pain, suffering, and death. The reason God hates these seven evil things is that they all harm people made in his image. The hatred of God is motivated by the love of God.

God hates not only evil behavior, but also evil people, specifically a person who stirs up conflict (Prov 6:19). And while it isn't a major theme, this divine hatred of evil people shows up elsewhere in the Old Testament. God hates all evildoers (Ps 5:5). God's soul hates those who love violence (Ps 11:5). Because of the evilness and wickedness of people, God began to hate them (Hos 9:15). Let's look at a specific example.

WHY DID GOD HATE ESAU?

Sometimes God's hate seems random. The book of Malachi includes this confusing declaration from God: "I have loved Jacob, but Esau I have hated (*sana'*)" (Mal 1:2-3). Jacob and Esau were the twin sons of Isaac and Rebekah, and the grandsons of Abraham and Sarah (Gen 25:19-26). Why did God hate Esau?

To address a difficult question like this, the broader context of Scripture helps us. Anyone who has read about the patriarchs and matriarchs of Genesis knows that they had messed up families.[4] But the relevant issue here is that father Isaac loved the older son Esau, while mother Rebekah loved the younger son Jacob (Gen 25:28), a prototypical example of bad parenting. But as we move to Malachi, it gets worse.

Through the prophet Malachi, Yahweh first tells Israel, "I have loved you," which prompts them to ask, "How have you loved us?" (Mal 1:2). To prove his love for his people, Yahweh brings up Jacob and Esau, specifically how he loved the younger son Jacob and hated the older son Esau. How are these ancient ancestors of the Israelites relevant in Malachi's fifth century context? Let's return to Genesis. After an all-night wrestling match with God, Jacob is renamed "Israel," which means "God-wrestler."[5] Jacob's descendants become the nation of Israel, and Esau's descendants became the nation of Edom (Gen 25:23, 30; 36:1, 8). In Malachi, Jacob and Esau refer not to the original twins, but to their descendants, the nations of Israel and Edom.

What does the text mean here when it says God hated Esau (i.e., Edom)? There are three options for understanding *hate* in Malachi 1; one looks back to Genesis, one looks forward to Romans, and one focuses on the context here in Malachi.

First, **hate** *could mean that Yahweh loves Esau less than he loves Jacob.* This perspective is clearly seen in Genesis. Esau was a flawed person. He despised his birthright (Gen 25:29-34) and hated and planned to kill his brother (Gen 27:41). But God still loved Esau. Yahweh promised that Esau would become a nation (Gen 25:23), and his descendants became the nation of Edom (Gen 36). Isaac declared that Esau would serve his brother, but also that he would also throw off his brother's yoke (Gen 27:40). Jacob and Esau were reconciled, and Jacob presented his older brother with gifts of livestock, but Esau replied that he had abundant possessions, presumably received as a blessing from God (Gen 33:9). Moving beyond Genesis, after the Israelites were wandering in the wilderness, God commanded his people to not attack the Edomites, since he had given them the land of Seir as their possession (Deut 2:4-6). When Joshua set up the tribal borders of Israel they did not extend into the land of Edom (Josh 15:1, 21). It is clear that God blessed the person Esau and the nation Edom. Based on these texts it is reasonable to say, "God loved Esau less than he loved Jacob," but that's not the primary point of Malachi 1:2-3.

Second, **hate** *could mean that Yahweh did not choose Esau in the same way he chose Jacob.* In a covenantal context *hate* can mean "not choose," which is the point Paul makes when he quotes Malachi 1:2-3 in Romans 9:13. Paul explains that only Abraham's descendants through Isaac are his "true descendants" (Rom 9:6-12). Similarly, not all of Isaac's descendants are chosen. Before they were born, God selected the older (Esau) to serve the younger (Jacob; Rom 9:12; Gen 25:23), which leads to the quotation from Malachi 1:2-3. To be loved is to be selected by God (Jacob), to be hated is to be rejected by God (Esau).[6] From Romans 9, we can say hate means rejection, but that's not the primary point of Malachi 1:2-3.[7]

Third, **hate** *could mean that God judged Edom.* The focus in Malachi 1 isn't that Esau is loved less (as it is in Genesis), or that he is rejected (as it is in Romans 9), but that the descendants of Esau, the Edomites, are being punished. One could argue that punishment involves a reduction in love, or a rejection of sorts, but neither of those interpretations are emphasized in Malachi. Let's look at the immediate context.

> A prophecy: The word of the LORD to Israel through Malachi.
> "I have loved you," says the LORD.
> "But you ask, 'How have you loved us?'"
> "Was not Esau Jacob's brother?" declares the LORD. "Yet I have loved Jacob, but Esau I have hated, and I have turned his hill country into a wasteland and left his inheritance to the desert jackals."

Edom may say, "Though we have been crushed, we will re-build the ruins."

But this is what the LORD Almighty says: "They may build, but I will demolish. They will be called the Wicked Land, a people always under the wrath of the LORD. You will see it with your own eyes and say, 'Great is the LORD—even beyond the borders of Israel!'" (Mal 1:1-5)

There are three punishments listed here. Yahweh turned their hill country into a wasteland, Yahweh left their inheritance to jackals (the land Yahweh gave them initially; Deut 2:4-6), and Yahweh is going to demolish their rebuilt ruins. The reason for the divine judgment is that they are evil. It would be truly disturbing if God brought these consequences down upon Edom merely because they weren't chosen. The reason they are called "Wicked Land" isn't be-cause God is making them wicked—they were already wicked. They are under the wrath of Yahweh because they have been committing evil deeds. The books of Amos and Obadiah describe the hatred, lack of compassion, and mistreatment that Edom showed toward their "brother" Jacob (Amos 1:11; Obad 1:10-14; see also Is 34:5-9; Jer 49:7-22; Ezek 25:12-14).

Hatred is used in Malachi as a synonym for judgment—"Esau I have judged." From the Pentateuch one could argue that God loved Esau less, and from Romans, one could argue that God rejected Esau, but in Malachi 1 God judges Edom because of their evilness. This fits the pattern we've been seeing elsewhere in the Old Testament. God's hatred is motivated by his love. He hates it when people are being harmed or oppressed. God doesn't sit by and dispassionately witness evil behavior. It prompts an emotional response of hatred, which leads him to judge and then to punish.

While judgment is still troubling, two points make it less so. First, we can rejoice that justice is accomplished when evil is judged, just as the Nazis were condemned at the Nuremberg trials. For any of us who have been victimized by evil, the confidence that it will be judged by God helps us process and heal from the incident and can serve to validate our pain. Second, as we see in the rest of Malachi, God is willing to withhold judgment when people repent (Mal 3:5-7; 4:5-6). When people ask for mercy, God's hate is overcome by his love.

"I HATE THEM WITH COMPLETE HATRED"

God hates evil behavior and evil doers, but is it appropriate for the people of God to hate? Perhaps surprisingly, many of the Old Testament "haters" appear in the book of Psalms. Psalms mentions not only evil people who hate good (Ps 41:7; 44:7; 69:4; 81:15), but also good people who hate evil (Ps 26:5; 31:6; 97:10; 119:113). The psalmists pray through their hatred, giving their feelings of animosity over to a God who knows when it is time to hate and time to love.

Psalm 139 is well-loved by many Christians. It describes how God knows us, how God's Spirit is always with us, and how God made us fearfully and wonderfully (vv. 1, 7, 14). But the end of the psalm may be less familiar, as the tone becomes darker, moving into imprecation, a prayer of cursing.

> Oh that you would slay the wicked, O God!
>> O men of blood, depart from me!
> They speak against you with malicious intent;
>> your enemies take your name in vain.
> Do I not hate those who hate you, O LORD?
>> And do I not loathe those who rise up against you?
> I hate (*sana'*) them with complete hatred (*sin'ah*);
>> I count them my enemies.
> Search me, O God, and know my heart!
>> Try me and know my thoughts!

And see if there be any grievous way in me,

and lead me in the way everlasting! (Ps 139:19-24 ESV)

After praying for judgment upon the wicked, the psalmist expresses hatred for people who hate God (who apparently weren't "fearfully and wonderfully made"). In the spirit of "an eye for an eye" (Ex 21:24; Lev 24:20), the text repeats how the psalmist hates God-haters four times in two verses (Ps 139:21-22). The behaviors that provoke the psalmist's hatred include general wickedness, as well as crimes involving violence, malicious speech, and swearing falsely. This psalm seems to be saying that people who hate God deserve hatred in return.

Many of us would feel uncomfortable praying a prayer of imprecation like this. (I dare you to start your next prayer meeting with "Slay the wicked, O God! I hate them with complete hatred.") Isn't the psalmist's hate just as bad as the hatred of these evildoers? The hate of the psalmist may appear similar to that of the God-hater, but three things distinguish these hatreds.

First, the object of the wicked person's hate is a righteous God, while the object of the psalmist's hate are evil people. The object of the hate matters. Evil people hate God because he punishes their wicked behavior. God restricts their ability to do harm. Their hatred is motivated by selfishness. God hates and punishes the wicked because their violence and deception is harming others ("malicious intent"), and they want to continue doing so without consequences. The psalmist's hatred is motivated by righteousness.

Second, after the imprecation the psalmist asks God for heart purification, to make sure it is in the right place.[8] Psalm 139 ends where it began with the theme of God searching the heart of the psalmist. However, instead of a declaration like at the beginning ("You have searched me and known me," v. 1), there is a petition at the end ("Search me and know my heart," v. 23). If we move into praying judgment upon others, we need God to help us make sure our heart is motivated by justice, not vengeance.

Third, the only thing we know that the psalmist is doing here in response to the hatred is praying. The God-haters were violent and deceptive, but the psalm mentions no violence, deception, or other actions taken against these evildoers, only prayer. The psalmist expects God first to search motives, then to judge, and finally to punish. To be clear here, the psalmist isn't passive. Hatred motivates the prayer. If one truly believes God is sovereign, the most powerful action one can take to stop evil and wickedness is to cry out to a God who hates evil behavior.

The hatred of the psalmist is completely different from that of the God-haters. Just as God's hatred is motivated by love, so is the hatred of the psalmist here. These differences allow people of faith to appropriate a prayer like this. We may feel uncomfortable with the intensity of the emotions in these imprecatory psalms, but the psalmist knew that God was comfortable with intense emotions because he is an intensely emotional God.

When I am struggling to make sense of the racism and sexism, the violence and oppression of our world, I find praying like the psalmist here—even though it makes me uncomfortable—helps me. It gives me hope, as I give over my anger and hatred to my God, who is righteous. He will search me and know my heart, and he will judge wickedness in order to protect those who have been victims of evil actions.

THE HATRED OF JESUS

Perhaps more so than any other figure in history, Jesus is identified with love. And yet even Jesus spoke about hate. He told his disciples in the Olivet discourse, "You will be *hated* (*miseō*) by all for my name's sake" (Lk 21:17 ESV). Why would his followers be hated? For the same reason that Jesus was hated (Lk 6:22; Jn 15:18-19; 1 Jn 3:13). Jesus testified that the works of the world are evil (Jn 3:20; 7:7). He called out religious hypocrisy (Mt 23; Mk 12). He defamed idols of power, money, and materialism (Lk 12:13-33; 16:19-31; 18:18-30). He confronted injustice and oppression (Mt 25:31-46; Mk 10:35-45; 11:15-19). He hated evil. And he expected his followers to do the same, so he knew they would be hated.

But Jesus didn't just say his followers would be hated, he told them to hate as well. "If anyone comes to me and does not hate (*miseō*) his own father and mother and wife and children and brothers and sisters, yes, and even his own life, he cannot be my disciple" (Lk 14:26 ESV; see also Jn 12:25). Is Jesus really telling us we need to hate our parents?

While I don't think that was what *hate* meant in Malachi 1, here I think it means "to love less." The command to love our neighbor (Lev 19:18), which Jesus said was one of the two greatest command-ments (Mk 12:28-34), would presumably apply to our parents, our children, and our siblings: the people Jesus seems to tell us to hate here. Jesus tells his followers to hate even themselves (Lk 14:26; Jn 12:25). But within his command to love neighbors is a command to love yourself. And this command is repeated not only in the Gospels (Mt 19:19; 22:39; Mk 12:31, 33; Lk 10:27), but also elsewhere in the New Testament (Rom 13:9; Gal 5:14; Jas 2:8). There's a time to hate, but we are called to spend far more time loving than hating. Christians should be known for their love, not their hate.

Why does Jesus use the word *hate*? Jesus' provocative use of this hyperbolic language gets our attention. It's shocking. In this context, it causes us to rethink our priorities. I know many college students have felt God was leading them into summer mission's projects or into a career in ministry that their parents didn't approve of. Their parents may perceive their decision to be disrespectful, perhaps even hateful. They still love their parents, but they love them less than they love Jesus. Intense love for Jesus and desire to follow him at all costs could look like hatred to friends and family who don't share this commitment.

In one other New Testament text, Jesus speaks of hatred. He tells the church in Ephesus, "Yet this you have: you hate (*miseō*) the works of the Nicolaitans, which I also hate (*miseō*)" (Rev 2:6). It is difficult to be certain what the Nicolaitans were doing that provoked hatred, but scholars assume they were a heretical sect involved in immorality, false teaching, and eating food offered to idols.[9] Jesus not only shared the Ephesians' hatred of the Nicolaitans' deeds, but he also affirmed the Ephesians for their animosity. Hatred of evil behavior thus characterized God and God's people in both the Old and the New Testament.

HATE THE SIN AND HATE THE SINNER?

When the topic of hating evil comes up, someone will often say, "Hate the sin, but love the sinner." There is much truth in this statement. We should focus on loving sinners, and we should resist sinful behavior. But I see three problems with it.

First, the saying has become a cliché. When an expression is overused, it loses its power. It becomes trite. Jesus never used platitudes but spoke in provocative language (hate your family), turning familiar expressions on their head, perhaps most famously in the Sermon on the Mount ("You have heard that it was said . . . but I say to you"; Mt 5:21, 27, 33, 38, 43). Jesus' provocative language gets our attention and forces us to think differently. Clichés have the opposite impact—"I've heard that before"—and we tune out. When people hear an overly familiar expression like this one, it has little affect.

Second, the saying suggests some people are especially bad sinners, unlike the rest of us who are called to love them. It is usually expressed in contexts that focus on sinful people who are different from us, often people we may find difficult to love. If we are poor, it may be on folks who we perceive to be rich (greed). If we are thin, it may be on folks who we perceive to be overweight (gluttony). If we work hard, it may be on folks who we perceive to be lazy (sloth). But perhaps, the most common usage of this saying is in contexts where straight people are talking about people who are gay, which is the point pastor Adam Hamilton makes in his book, *Half Truths*, where he discusses this saying.[10] Instead of this cliché, Hamilton thinks Jesus would say, "Love your neighbor despite the fact that you are a sinner."

Third, the saying not only isn't found it Scripture, it contradicts what Scripture teaches. While we don't really see hate of sinners in the New Testament, the Old Testament clearly speaks of God and the people of God hating sinners. Jesus also tells us to hate people that could get in the way of our relationship with him. Although, we now realize that in his context, Jesus means love them less. Hamilton believes the only true part of the saying is the word *love*. I completely agree that we need to focus on love. But both the Old and New Testament emphasize that we are called to hate sin.

One could argue that there's biblical support for a new saying: "Hate the sin and hate the sinner," but it would be a mistake to repeat something like that. It is too easily misconstrued, and it puts too much emphasis on the hate. There are churches that are known for their public declarations stating "God hates . . ." groups of people whom they deem to be worse sinners than they are. They are missing the point. God hates people who harm others. The hatred of these "God-hates" churches often targets people who are already marginalized, the very people that God extends love and mercy toward.

But we do need to understand how the Bible wants us to hate appropriately. Because we love God, and our neighbor, we hate sin. How do we do that? Jesus shows us.

RESIST EVIL

One way to understand what appropriate hate looks like is to think about resistance. The books of James and 1 Peter command readers to resist the devil (Jas 4:7; 1 Pet 5:9), which sounds like what the psalmist was doing in Psalm 139, praying judgment upon God-haters.

The problem with this idea is that Jesus said, "Do not resist (*anthistēmi*) the one who is evil" (Mt 5:39). How do we reconcile these apparently contradictory biblical commands—should we resist or not resist evil? Once again, Jesus gives us the answer. At the most critical point in his life, Jesus did not resist evil when he was betrayed, arrested, interrogated, beaten, and crucified (Mk 14:43–15:37). Because Jesus didn't resist evil, he died for the sins of the world. But over the course of his life Jesus also resisted evil as he overturned tables, condemned religious hypocrisy, and warned against greed, lust, and pride (Mt 5:27-30; 6:19-21; Mk 11:15–12:44; Lk 12:13-21; 16:19-31; 18:9-14, 18-30).

When Jesus resisted evil, was he not following his own advice in the Sermon on the Mount? No. Just as he used hyperbole to tell his followers to hate their parents, he uses hyperbole here to make the point about not resisting evil. His provocative language gets our attention and forces us to reflect on when and why we need to resist or not resist. Just as there is a time to hate and a time to love, there is also a time to resist and a time not to resist.

"SHALL I SHOOT?"

The life of Dietrich Bonhoeffer offers wisdom as we struggle to know when to resist or not resist evil (Bonhoeffer has a cameo in the book *Resistance Women*, mentioned at the beginning of this chapter). In Bonhoeffer's discussion of Matthew 5:38-42 from the Sermon on the Mount, he advocates for non-resistance: "The only way to overcome evil is to let it run itself to a standstill because it does not find the resistance it is looking for."[11] And yet, faced with the evils of the Nazi regime, Bonhoeffer was actively involved in the resistance movement serving as a courier to Western Allies and helping German Jews escape to Switzerland.[12]

In the fall of 1941 Bonhoeffer told a group of his fellow conspirators that, if necessary, he would be willing to kill Hitler. In the fall

of 1942 Bonhoeffer was asked by Werner von Haeften, the younger
brother of one of his former seminary students, "Shall I shoot? I can
get inside the Führer's headquarters with my revolver. I know where
and when the conferences take place." Bonhoeffer's internal struggle
with this issue is seen in his reply, that von Haeften needed to make
that decision for himself. Bonhoeffer's lack of rebuke was interpreted
as permission by von Haeften. By not reporting him to the author-
ities, Bonhoeffer was committing treason and resisting the evil of
the Nazis.

Von Haeften was the adjutant to Colonel Claus von Stauffenberg,
who led the July 20, 1944, assassination attempt against Hitler, portrayed in the 2008 film *Valkyrie* (starring Tom Cruise as Stauffenberg).
Von Haeften helped Stauffenberg plant the briefcase bomb near
Hitler (he "shot"), which did not kill the dictator. Many of the conspirators were executed the same night. Both in real life and in the
film version, as the firing squad was about to shoot, von Haeften
rushed in front of Stauffenberg to take his bullet, one final act of
resistance to evil.

THE ARMOR OF GOD

Paul provides a helpful metaphor for understanding the appropriateness of resistance when he tells the Ephesians to "take up the
full armor of God, that you may be able to resist (*anthistēmi*) in
the evil day" (Eph 6:13 NASB 1995). The same verb for *resist* in
Ephesians 6 (*anthistēmi*) is used for resist in Jesus's command to
"not resist" (Mt 5:39).

God's armor will allow the Ephesians to resist the "schemes of
the devil . . . the spiritual forces of evil . . . the evil one" (Eph 6:11,
12, 16). Most of the armor is defensive (the belt, the breastplate,
the shoes, the shield, and the helmet), but the sword of the Spirit
is offensive—used to attack evil. There were decades between
when Paul first wrote this letter and when John wrote his letter to

the church in Ephesus (Rev 2:1-7). During this period, the Ephesians apparently learned how to utilize their armor of God and wield their sword of the Spirit in their hatred of the actions of Nicolaitans (Rev 2:6).

OUR GOD IS A GOD OF HATE

Part of our discomfort with these divine hatred texts is that the God of love is also a God of hate. But the problem is deeper than that. If Scripture merely said God judged evil, few would be troubled by that. Wicked behavior needs to be judged, and who better to do that than a righteous God?

The deeper problem is that evil behavior affects God emotionally. He doesn't just punish evildoers, he hates them. Evil behavior elicits a highly negative emotional response from the God of the universe. God cannot remain dispassionate about wickedness.

While this divine behavior may disturb us, it should reassure us. Imagine how you would feel if someone were physically striking a beloved family member—punching your daughter or son, beating up your spouse, attacking your parent—how would you feel? Would it be good for this evil behavior to not affect you? We would call someone with no emotions at this point cold-blooded, dispassionate, non-human. The fact that the God of the universe is affected by evil—he hates it—means that he cares deeply. Ultimately, he hates intensely because he loves intensely.

WHAT SHOULD WE HATE?

What should we hate? God is not calling us to hate inconvenience, rudeness, or flying. God never calls us to hate ourselves. To people who struggle with self-hatred, God says, You are made in my image (Gen 1:26-27). You are fearfully and wonderfully made (Ps 139:14). Love yourself, just as you love your neighbor (Lev 19:18; Mk 12:31). God loves his people and wants us to love ourselves.

God and the people of God focus their hatred on violence, deception, pride, a lack of compassion, and oppression. In a word, wickedness. It is easy to become numb to the evils that surround us. We have become immune to the depravity of sin. We should be appalled. But as the people of God love the things that God loves, as followers of Jesus love what Jesus loves, we will hate hatred and evil. It should evoke strong emotions of loathing and revulsion. Injustice should make us sick. Greed should disgust us. Racism should cause us to scream. Sexual abuse should make us furious. What do we do with these emotions? Three things come to mind.

Expressing hatred in prayer. First, we should express our hatred of injustice to God in prayer. I joked about it earlier, but we seriously need to add imprecatory language into our personal and corporate prayers. Prayer journaling could be a safe space to practice using hyperbolic language like that of the psalmist in Psalm 139. Or try sharing some of your intense emotions with others as you pray, "I hate them with complete hatred." Yelling during a prayer meeting would be memorable, and would keep people awake. Lately, while blessing the food before dinner, I have been praying imprecation against systems of injustice and national leaders who don't seem to care about justice, greed, racism, or abuse.

Teaching imprecatory prayer. Second, we should study and teach imprecatory prayers or parts of the Bible that speak of God's hatred toward evil, injustice, and oppression. When topics for sermons, Sunday school classes, or small groups are being decided, texts that address the hatred of God are often ignored. We should teach on the parts of Scripture that address sexual abuse and then pray imprecatory prayers against perpetrators. Obviously, we want perpetrators to stop victimizing, to repent, and get connected to Jesus, but we will trust God to decide the best way to do that. For people who have been sexually abused, an important initial step of healing may be to pray honestly to God about how they feel about their abuser. Instead of forcing a victim prematurely toward forgiveness, giving them time to express raw emotions, following the example of the psalmist, will allow them to eventually forgive in a healthy manner.

Getting involved in justice. Third, we should get involved in organizations that address injustice or oppression. It's good to pray and study Scripture, but our intense emotions need to be channeled into helpful directions. We need to find creative ways to resist evil. There is too much evil in the world, and we aren't called to fix all of it. But my guess is that God is calling you to get involved in an issue that you feel passionately about (racism, sexual abuse, abortion, poverty, the environment, injustice, etc.). Take a step in the next week to get involved.

RESISTING EVIL

People who have been victims of hate crimes will naturally respond with hatred. Returning to *Resistance Women*, the setting is now about ten years later (1940). As the Allies are bombing Berlin, Sara's brother Natan suggests painting on their roof, "Jews here," so the British would know to drop bombs elsewhere. He continues, "Why should [the British] kill us? We hate the Nazis even more than they do."[13] The women (and men) of *Resistance Women* were motivated by their hatred of the Nazis to risk their lives helping Jews get out of Germany and to pass on vital information to the Allies. Just as Nazi hatred of Jews provoked these women to resist, so should contemporary forms of oppression, injustice, and racism provoke hatred in us, motivating us to resist evil.

THE HATE MAN

In the 1960s Mark Hawthorne was a reporter with the *New York Times*. But starting in the early 1970s he lived homeless in Berkeley, California. He wanted people to express negativity, because he believed it was more honest than positive expressions or flattery. To start a conversation with him, you needed to say, "I hate you." He became known as the Hate Man, or sometimes just "Hate."[14] (I doubt his parents called him that.) While Christians should be known for their love, not their hate, we could learn from him about honesty and healthy expressions of resistance in relationships. He was opposed to most forms of religion, but he would have loved the honesty of the imprecatory psalms.

One day, I had an encounter with the Hate Man.

When I was on InterVarsity staff in Southern California, each May we'd take a group of students to an evangelism project in Berkeley. Over the course of ten days, students talked about Jesus to people, both college students and the many folks in Berkeley who were experiencing homelessness.

One year I felt God was calling me to try open-air preaching. I had never done it before, but God gave me a loud voice, so I thought I should put it to good use. Sproul Plaza at Berkeley was the birthplace of the Free Speech Movement in the 1960s and it always attracted local open-air preachers, many of whom wore sandwich boards proclaiming "Turn or burn!" Needless to say, students either ignored or ridiculed these preachers. Kirk, a student in our group, was brave enough to join me in this adventure.

Kirk and I went out to Sproul Plaza at noon on a beautiful spring day. There were hundreds of students enjoying the sun and eating their lunch. And scattered around were homeless folks, looking for handouts. Instead of sandwich boards and a "Turn or burn!" message, Kirk and I decided to simply retell some of Jesus' parables: the prodigal son, the Good Samaritan, the rich man and Lazarus.

I was nervous. I started out, "There was a man who had two sons. The younger son came up and said, 'Hey, Dad, I want my half of the inheritance now'..." As I was talking, the Hate Man suddenly appeared.

There were few things the Hate Man loved more than heckling open-air preachers. He would literally get in your face and yell. He would point out the hypocrisy of these preachers (often with a valid point). Berkeley students loved to watch the spectacle. A preacher would start preaching, then students would see the Hate Man emerge from the edge of the crowd and they would say, "Here we go. The Hate Man cometh."

But Kirk and I knew what to expect because Roger, another student on our project, had spent time listening to and befriending the Hate Man. We had heard Roger's stories and had been praying daily for the Hate Man. We knew how to communicate with him. The Hate Man told Roger people needed to express negativity by gently pushing their hand against someone when they didn't like what the other person was doing.

As the Hate Man rushed up to heckle me, my partner Kirk went to the Hate Man and put his hand up to push. The Hate man paused. And then he put his hand up and pushed. They stood with their hands together. No preachers had ever done this before.

But the Hate Man really hated preachers. The hand pushing wasn't enough, so Kirk started to lean his whole body against him (Roger told us about this too). The Hate Man stopped and listened quietly. They leaned. I preached. After ten minutes, I concluded, "The father said, 'This son of mine was dead and now is alive; he was lost and is found!'" Then I traded places with Kirk, leaning against the Hate Man, as Kirk took my spot and retold another parable. We alternated preaching and leaning.

While we were speaking, our friends on the project asked people sitting next to them, "What do you think about what these guys are saying about Jesus?" "It's interesting, but how did they get the Hate Man to stay quiet?" "God moves in mysterious ways."

In our relationships, it is often tempting to respond to hate with hate, or in this instance, to heckling with heckling. But the love of God compels us toward love, and toward resisting evil in a loving way. While the Hate Man might say we were hating him by pushing, by leaning, I would say we were loving him, by listening to him, and communicating in ways he understood. We resisted his efforts to shut us down, because we wanted people, including him, to hear about the love of God.

3

the wrath of god

My wrath will burn and I will kill you with the sword.

EXODUS 22:21

A WHILE AGO I WAS INVITED to write an article on *wrath* for an IVP Bible dictionary.[1] I'd like to think that I was selected for the topic because I wrote about God's anger in *God Behaving Badly*—chapter two asked, "Is God angry or loving?"—not due to something the dictionary editors knew about my temperament.[2]

Shortly after being asked to write on wrath, another friend invited me to contribute an article to a volume he was helping put together on holy warfare in ancient Israel. I said, "How about an emotional take on warfare: compassion and wrath?" My friend said, "You're a man of wrath, so that's a go."[3]

Since I was getting a reputation for being the wrath-of-God guy, when the chance came to speak at my church, I spoke on God's wrath, based on my book. Over the past ten years, what topic have I preached about more than any other? Divine wrath, of course. I preached on wrath again just last week.

In the midst of this period of obsession with divine anger, I went golfing with friends one day. The same day Tiger Woods shot a 77 at the PGA (August 11, 2011), I shot a 65 (but I only played nine holes).

My friend Jesse looked at my clubs, and said, "What's this? It says 'WRATH' on your golf club. The Wrath of Dave!" Even my golf clubs associate me with wrath.[4] As we'll see in this chapter, God is also associated with wrath.

DEFINING WRATH

Anger is defined as a strong feeling of annoyance, antagonism, or displeasure resulting from a grievance or opposition. While anger is already a strong emotion, wrath takes it up a notch, understood as violent anger, rage, or fury. On Robert Plutchik's wheel of emotions the process of emotional escalation for anger synonyms goes from annoyance to anger and then rage. While there are differences in how the Bible uses these various terms (e.g., wrath is often associated with judgment), in this chapter I will speak of wrath and anger almost synonymously.

While Yoda in *Star Wars: The Phantom Menace* famously said, "Anger leads to hate," in this book the order is flipped.[5] How is anger distinct from hatred? Both are strong negative emotions, but hatred is deeper and tends to last longer. The Nazis hatred of the Jews survived decades, and God's hatred of evil behavior is permanent. Anger, however, is often triggered by a specific action, the person who cut us off on the road. There is a reason it's called *road rage*, not *road hate*. Just as anger rises quickly, it can also subside quickly. Because of its duration hatred can be more powerful, but because of its intensity anger can be harder to control.

WORDS OF WRATH

As we examine the words the Bible uses for anger, we discover that, more than any other divine emotion except perhaps love, the God of the Bible is a God of wrath. To display the variety of wrath words in Scripture, I've constructed two tables with examples and references. Table 3.1 lists eight Hebrew words used to connote divine wrath in the Old Testament.

Table 3.1. Wrath in the Old Testament

Hebrew	English	Divine anger examples (ESV) (emphasis added)	Other references
'anap	to be angry	How long, O LORD? Will you be **angry** forever (Ps 79:5)?	Deut 1:37; 1 Kings 8:46; Is 12:1
'ap	anger	Then the **anger** the LORD was kindled against Moses (Ex 4:14).	Num 11:1; Ps 2:5; Jer 4:8
ka'as	to provoke to anger	They went after other gods . . . they provoked the LORD to **anger** (Judg 2:12).	Deut 4:25; 1 Kings 14:9; Jer 7:18
harah	to burn (with anger)	Yahweh: My wrath will **burn**, and I will kill you with the sword (Ex 22:23).	Job 42:7; 2 Sam 6:7; Is 5:25
qatsap	to be indignant	Yahweh: I was **angry** with my people, I profaned my heritage (Is 47:6).	Deut 1:34; Josh 22:18; Eccles 5:6
hemah	wrath	For great is the **wrath** of the LORD that is kindled against us (2 Kings 22:13).	Deut 29:23; 2 Chron 12:7; Mic 5:15
'ebrah	wrath	He let loose on them his burning anger, **wrath**, indignation, and distress (Ps 78:49).	Is 10:6; Jer 7:29; Hab 3:8
za'ap	rage, indignation	I will bear the **indignation** of the LORD because I have sinned against him (Mic 7:9).	Is 30:30

Table 3.2 lists seven Greek words used to connote wrath in the New Testament. Not all of these New Testament examples of anger are connected with God.

Table 3.2. Wrath in the New Testament

Greek	English	Anger examples (ESV)[6] (emphasis added)	Other references
orgē	wrath	You brood of vipers! Who warned you to flee from the **wrath** to come (Mt 3:7)?	Jn 3:36; Rom 1:18; Rev 6:16;
orgizō	to be angry	And in **anger** his master[7] delivered him to the jailers (Matt 18:34).	Lk 14:21
thymos	anger	He also will drink the wine of God's **wrath** (Rev 14:10).	Rev 15:1; 16:1; 19:15
aganakteō	to be indignant, angry	But when Jesus saw it, he was **indignant** and said to them, "Let the children come to me" (Mk 10:14).	Mt 20:24; 21:15; 26:8; Mk 10:14; Lk 13:14

Greek	English	Anger examples (ESV)[6] (emphasis added)	Other references
orgilos	angry	For an overseer, as God's steward . . . must not be arrogant or **quick-tempered** (Titus 1:7).	
parorgismos	anger	Do not let the sun go down on your **anger** (Eph 4:26).	
cholaō	to be angry	Are you **angry** with me because on the Sabbath I made a man's whole body well (Jn 7:23)?	

Many of these Hebrew and Greek words appear dozens of times throughout the Bible, particularly in the Old Testament. The English words *anger*, *angry*, and *wrath* appear 575 times in the ESV translation, almost as frequently as the words *love* and *compassion* appear (603 times in the ESV). The vast majority of these biblical references are to the anger or wrath of God. The early twentieth-century Bible teacher A. W. Pink states, "A study of the concordance will show that there are more references in Scripture to the anger, fury and wrath of God than there are to his love and tenderness."[8] God gets angry a lot.

We may feel more comfortable emphasizing God is a God of love, but according to Scripture, we could just as easily say he is a God of anger. While his propensity toward wrath may be deeply troubling, as we examine these references to understand how and why God gets angry, his behavior will not only make sense, it will be worthy of praise.

ANGER, IT GETS THE JOB DONE

In *Star Wars: Revenge of the Sith*, as Anakin Skywalker confronts Emperor Palpatine and is planning to kill him, Palpatine attempts to seduce Anakin to the dark side of "the force" by encouraging him to channel his anger (spoiler alert).

Palpatine to Anakin: "Are you going to kill me?"

Anakin: "I would certainly like to."

Palpatine: "I know you would. I can feel your anger. It gives you focus, makes you stronger."

Not only can he shoot lightning from his fingers, Palpatine also understands something profound about anger. It gives power. As the Star Wars saga continues, Anakin transforms into Darth Vader,[9] his rage-fueled mastery of the force is unassailable and he crushes opponents and even subordinate officers who disappoint him (like Captain Needa, "apology accepted"). In *The Empire Strikes Back*, just as he was seduced by Palpatine during a confrontation, Vader encourages Luke Skywalker to give in to his anger and join him (before he reveals to Luke, "I am your father!").[10]

Vader to Luke: "Obi-Wan has taught you well. You have controlled your fear. Now . . . release your anger. Only your hatred can destroy me."[11]

While there is a lot to critique about it, the Star Wars franchise appropriately realizes the power of emotions. Anger, in particular, is an emotion of power. The intensity of wrath gets people's attention; it prompts people to action. Football coaches use anger to inspire their team at halftime to make a furious comeback in the second half. Military leaders channel anger to challenge their forces to risk their lives to attack the enemy. The anger of many a parent has motivated a lazy child to do their chores around the house. Anger, it gets the job done. But is it good?

ANGER: GOOD OR BAD?

Anger can be good or bad, depending on the job that needs to get done. Selfish anger is focused on wrong done to oneself, often prompted by inconvenience or insult. This type of anger can be used to control or manipulate others. Someone yells at members of their family to interrupt them, to shut down dissenting views, or to retaliate against someone who has insulted them.

While the anger that Palpatine fostered in Anakin started out as a desire to protect Padme, the woman he loves, it becomes an obsession with control, hatred, and power. However, if anger is a response to evil and it focuses on wrongs done to others, it is more likely to be righteous. Righteous anger can motivate people to mobilize and bring down systems of injustice (e.g., #MeToo or Black Lives Matter).

Paul focuses on the downside of anger as he includes it among the works of the flesh (Gal 5:20). Anger is not one of the fruits of the Spirit, but it is an emotion that both Yahweh in the Old Testament and Jesus in the New display frequently. As we examine what God gets angry about, we'll see his anger is righteous.

WHY DOES GOD GET ANGRY A LOT?

This chapter won't be able to look at all the hundreds of texts describing divine anger, but table 3.3 lists five of the primary causes that are repeated throughout Scripture (oppression, evil, violence, disobedience, and idolatry). The table includes a sample verse and several other references where the specific cause appears.

Table 3.3. Causes for divine anger

Cause	Divine anger example (ESV)[12] (emphasis added)	Other references
Oppression	Thus says the LORD: "Execute justice in the morning, and deliver from the hand of the oppressor him who has been robbed, lest my **wrath** (*hemah*) go forth like fire" (Jer 21:12).	Ex 3:9-4:14; 22:21-24; 1 Kings 21:22; Ps 78:49; Is 10:2-4; Ezek 22:29-31; Zech 7:10-12
Evil	Those who plow iniquity and sow trouble reap the same. By the breath of God they perish, and by the blast of his **anger** (*'ap*) they are consumed (Job 4:8-9).	Deut 1:34-35; Prov 11:23; Job 4:8-9; Jer 30:23
Violence	I will make your house like the house of Jeroboam ... for the **anger** (*ka'as*) to which you have **provoked** (*ka'as*) me (1 Kings 21:22).	Jer 2:34-35; Ezek 24:12-14

Cause	Divine anger example (ESV)[12] (emphasis added)	Other references
Disobedience	Great is the **wrath** (*hemah*) of the LORD that is kindled against us, because our fathers have not obeyed the words of this book (2 Kings 22:13).	Josh 7:1; 22:20; Judg 2:20; Ps 78:21
Idolatry	They went after other gods, from among the gods of the peoples who were around them, and bowed down to them. And they provoked the LORD to **anger** (*ka'as*; Judg 2:12).	Ex 32:10-12; Num 25:3-4; 2 Chron 29:8; Ps 78:58; Jer 7:18; 8:19; 11:17

God gets angry about oppression whether his people are the victims or the perpetrators. We see God's wrath toward oppression throughout the Bible, but particularly in the prophetic books and Exodus. Evildoers also provoke the wrath of God, as seen in the passage from Job and elsewhere. The example of violence in the table comes from the judgment pronounced by Elijah against King Ahab and Queen Jezebel for arranging the death of innocent Naboth so Ahab can take possession of his vineyard (this reference is also cited under oppression). Disobedience also provokes the wrath of God as illustrated by King Josiah's speech to his officials in 2 Kings 22. The idolatry of God's people prompts divine anger as well as divine jealousy, so idolatry will also be discussed in the next chapter on the jealousy of God.

At this point we need to observe something that should be obvious, but often isn't mentioned. Human actions provoke God's anger.[13] The text makes it clear that the oppression, evil, violence, disobedience, and idolatry of humans is what prompts God's wrath. Anger is not intrinsic to God's divine character independent of the actions of humans. In his long address to the people on the plains of Moab, Moses reminds the Israelites of how they angered Yahweh, "Remember and do not forget how you provoked the LORD your God to wrath in the wilderness" (Deut 9:7 ESV). Many other texts describe how human behaviors lead to divine anger (Deut 4:25; 9:22;

32:16; Judg 2:12; 1 Kings 14:9; 2 Kings 21:6, 15; Is 65:3; Jer 7:18-19; Ezek 8:17; 16:26; Hos 12:14). According to the Bible, humans make God mad.

GOD'S ANGER IN EXODUS

Divine anger is a major theme in the book of Exodus, so we'll move there next. Moses is minding his own business, caring for the sheep of his father-in-law Jethro, when God speaks to him through a burning bush (Ex 3:1-4:17).[14] God tells Moses he has compassion on the Israelites, so he wants Moses to return to Egypt (Moses fled after killing an Egyptian; Ex 2:11-15) in order to bring his people out of Egypt. Yahweh counters each of Moses' first four objections, but after the fifth one he gets angry at the reluctant shepherd (Ex 4:14).

What prompted the divine anger? God wanted to deliver his people from oppression, but Moses was unwilling to help. This incident is the first time that Scripture records God becoming angry. Moses' lack of concern for the oppression of his own people prompted God to get mad here. As we'll soon see, God gets angry when his people oppress others, or don't help people who are oppressed. God's anger is righteous.

God had already revealed his power to Moses through the bush that perpetually burned, the staff that turned into a snake, and the hand that toggled leprosy (Ex 3:2-3; 4:3-4, 6-7), but none of these displays of supernatural power motivated Moses to return to Egypt. What finally squelched Moses' dissent and caused him to agree to help his oppressed fellow Israelites? The wrath of God. Anger, it gets the job done.

THE SNOT OF GOD'S WRATH

After the Egyptian pursuers are drowned in the Red Sea, Moses, his sister Miriam, and the nation celebrate their salvation on the seashore.

I will sing to the LORD, for he has triumphed gloriously;
the horse and his rider he has thrown into the sea.
> (Ex 15:1, 21 ESV)

In the middle of their song, they declare how God sent out his fury at the Egyptians to consume them (Ex 15:7). God's wrath targeted the nation of Egypt for oppressing his people for centuries. Verse 8 uses a beautiful image to describe this: the blast of God's nostrils piled up the water of the sea.

The Hebrew word used here, *'ap* (see table 3.1 of Hebrew anger words), can either mean "nose" or "anger," depending on the context. Here it means both. The *'ap* is not only blowing back water (God's nose must be pretty big to part the Red Sea), but it is also used in parallel with *fury* from the previous line. It's a Hebrew pun that's lost in English. God is shooting the snot of his wrath at the Egyptians, like a runner covers one nostril and blows out the other (I've only heard about this from others). God is an emotional God, an angry God, and his anger targets the oppressors. Once again, his anger is righteous.

We often feel uncomfortable with God's wrath. We ignore it, downplay it, or rationalize it. We think that an angry God is a God behaving badly. But according to Exodus 15, this emotional aspect of God's character, his divine wrath, should inspire not embarrassment but praise. Praise because it is wrath that leads to salvation for those who have been oppressed. Just like Moses and Miriam, we should sing about God's furious deliverance (big nostrils came in handy at the Red Sea).

THE DEADLY WRATH OF GOD

The next place the topic of divine anger appears in Exodus is in the context of the covenant code (Ex 21–23), which is a series of laws that God gave to the Israelites immediately after the Ten Commandments (Ex 20:1-17). These laws helped the Israelites practically

apply commandments 5–10, the "horizontal" ones focused on loving
their neighbor.

> You shall not wrong a sojourner or oppress him,
> for you were sojourners in the land of Egypt.
> You shall not mistreat any widow or fatherless child.
> If you do mistreat them, and (if) they cry out to me,
> I will surely hear their cry,
> and my wrath (*'ap*) will burn (*harah*),
> and I will kill you with the sword,
> and your wives shall become widows
> and your children fatherless. (Ex 22:21-24 ESV)

God first tells his people here not to wrong or oppress a sojourner
(basically a foreigner, or immigrant). God often gives commands
without a rationale, but he provides one here, emphasizing the importance of this command. Israel is not to oppress sojourners because they were sojourners in Egypt. The tragic reality is that people
who have been oppressed often become oppressors when they come
to power.[15]

Next, God commands his people to not mistreat widows and
orphans. For this command, God doesn't provide a reason, but he
does state the punishment. He warns them that his wrath will burn,
and it will burn so much that he will kill them with the sword. If
that weren't clear enough, he continues. Their wives will become
widows (he will kill them) and their children will become fatherless
(he will kill them).

Does that sound harsh? Perhaps. But it's only harsh toward people
who oppress the marginalized. People who should be afraid of this law
are those who exploit the weak, who don't show compassion to
children, single-mothers, foreigners, and immigrants. If you are a foreigner, a widow, or an orphan, this punishment isn't harsh at all. In a
world where the marginalized are accustomed to abuse, oppression,

and mistreatment, it's justice. It's a glorious command. It is something to be praised and sung about in the spirit of Exodus 15.

What motivates the justice here? God's wrath, which leads him to respond to the injustice. God does not sit idly by when marginalized people are being oppressed. It makes him mad. Why? Because he loves people. He loves the marginalized. When strong people mistreat weak people, God's ire is provoked.

But God even loves the oppressors by giving them this warning—you better care for widows, orphans, and foreigners—or else. They may feel mean, but warnings like Exodus 22 are acts of serious love. The intensity of this warning should motivate people who believe in God not only to not oppress the marginalized, but also to actively advocate on their behalf.

A death penalty judgment for oppression shouldn't surprise us. Paul says essentially the same thing when he states, "The wages of sin is death" (Rom 6:23). Fortunately, the God who gets mad at injustice is also quick to show mercy to repentant sinners: "We have now been justified by his blood, much more shall we be saved by him from the wrath of God" (Rom 5:9 ESV).

Does God still kill people who oppress the marginalized today? I don't know, and therefore I think the people of God need to be cautious about making pronouncements about catastrophes or weather-related tragedies that we might perceive as "an act of an angry God" against evildoers. But this is what I do know. The hyperbolic nature of the violent language of Exodus 22 gets my attention and should get the attention of anyone who is not actively attempting to care for and advocate for the marginalized, which often includes immigrants, women, minorities, children, and the disabled—roughly equivalent to the women, orphans, and foreigners that Scripture speaks of. Because God loves all people, the marginalized as well as the oppressors, he speaks frankly about his anger in order to motivate people to repent of their oppression and get involved in justice.

THE LONG NOSE OF THE LORD

In chapter four, which is on jealousy, we will look at God's anger at
the Israelites about the incident of the golden calf (Ex 32:10-12).
Here we'll examine the final time divine anger appears in Exodus,
when Yahweh reveals his name to Moses:

> Then the LORD came down in the cloud and stood there with
> him and proclaimed his name, the LORD. And he passed in front
> of Moses, proclaiming, "The LORD, the LORD, the compas-
> sionate and gracious God, slow to anger (*'ap*), abounding in love
> and faithfulness, maintaining love to thousands, and forgiving
> wickedness, rebellion and sin. Yet he does not leave the guilty
> unpunished; he punishes the children and their children for the
> sin of the parents to the third and fourth generation."(Ex 34:5-7)

While there are many things that could be said about this important passage where God reveals his name to Moses, I'll limit
myself to three observations.[16] First, emotional language dominates
this definition of God, both adjectives (compassionate and gracious),
as well as nouns (anger and love). God's emotional attributes aren't
merely felt, but they are expressed in his behaviors, seen particularly
in verse 7. Three of the emotions this book focuses on appear in this
section (anger, compassion, and love), and a fourth (jealousy) shows
up in a few verses (Ex 34:14). God's name emphasizes his emotions.

Second, since a name was meant to characterize a person, emotions characterize God. This was particularly true in the world of the
Bible. Jacob became Israel because he was the-one-who wrestles-
with-God (Gen 32:28). Simon wasn't just named Peter; he was the
rock upon which Jesus would build the church (Mt 16:18). God is
compassion. God is slowness to anger. God is abundant love. Emotions are a fundamental, not peripheral, aspect of God's character.

Third, this description of God's character comes from the mouth
of God himself. God uses highly emotive terms to introduce himself.

He is not embarrassed about his emotions—not even anger. But here and elsewhere he declares himself to be an emotional God. The Old Testament emphasizes God's emotions by repeating versions of this divine name revelation across its various genres, in law (Num 14:18), in history (Neh 9:17), in poetry (Ps 86:15; 103:8; 145:8), and in prophecy (Joel 2:13; Jon 4:2; Nah 1:3).

To return to the topic of divine anger, the expression *slow to anger* literally means "long-nosed." Once again, we see that God has a big nose (helpful when parting large bodies of water). Perhaps more so than any other emotion, anger is difficult to control, and yet that is exactly what God does. While humans are often quick to anger, God arrives there slowly. While God's anger is restricted, his love is unfettered—he abounds in love. And in Exodus particularly, God's anger targets oppression, both the oppressors and people who are unwilling to help end oppression. The anger of God is righteous.

GOD'S ANGER OVER RACISM AND INJUSTICE

In May 2020, my wife, Shannon, participated in a Civil Righteousness prayer event in Philadelphia on the steps of the art museum (not far from the Rocky statue), praying for justice and reconciliation in the light of recent killings of unarmed Black folks (Ahmaud Arbery, George Floyd). The group started praying in silence; then it slowly got dark. It began to rain. The wind blew. There was thunder and lightning. It was like what the Israelites experienced of God as they were at the foot of Mount Sinai (Ex 19:16), a few chapters before he warned them of his anger over injustice. Torrents of rain came hurtling down. Trees were literally flying through the air. It may have been pure coincidence, but it sure seemed like God was venting his anger about racism and injustice. The anger of God is righteous. (And Shannon's prayers are more powerful than mine; see James 5:16.)

THE WRATH OF JESUS

Despite the popular perception that the God of the Old Testament is angry while the God of the New Testament is loving, Jesus still gets quite angry. And, like Yahweh, Jesus' anger is motivated by love. In two instances Jesus gets mad when his ability to show compassion toward the marginalized is threatened. Before healing the man with the withered hand, Jesus was angry (*orgē*) and grieved at the hardness of heart of the religious leaders, who didn't want the man to be healed but were only concerned about Jesus healing on the Sabbath (Mk 3:5). Jesus was indignant (*aganakteō*) at his disciples for restricting the access of children since he wanted to welcome and bless them (Mk 10:14).

On two occasions the text doesn't explicitly state Jesus was angry, but he sure acts like it. When Jesus cleansed the temple, he flipped over the tables of the moneychangers and berated the religious leaders who allowed the temple to become a "den of robbers" (Mk 11:15-17). John's Gospel tells us he used a whip to drive out not only the animals, but also their humans (Jn 2:15). Jesus' anger targets the animal-sellers and moneychangers since their actions inhibited the prayers of the foreigners, since their transactions were taking place in the Court of Gentiles. Jesus specifically emphasizes his concern for the marginalized here as he states the temple was meant to be a "house of prayer for all the nations" (Mk 11:17). It is also hard not to assume Jesus was angry as he used harsh words against the scribes and the Pharisees, calling them a "brood of vipers" (Mt 23:33) and "hypocrites" six times (Mt 23:13, 15, 23, 25, 27, 29). Jesus' anger at the religious leaders was prompted by his concern for the crowds of people who were being misled by these leaders.

Wrath appears in the epistles of Paul (e.g., Rom 1:18; 2:5; 3:5; Eph 2:3; 4:31) and the book of Revelation (e.g., 11:18; 12:12; 16:19; 19:15) to primarily signify the judgment of God. While the seals of Revelation are being opened, everyone wants to be hidden from "the wrath of the Lamb" (Rev 6:16). (Personally, I am quite familiar with angry Lambs.)

THE WRATH OF GOD IN THE PARABLES OF JESUS

Two of Jesus' parables include a king who became angry. In the parable of the unforgiving servant (Mt 18:23-35), the king forgave one of his servants a massive debt. Then that servant found another servant who owed him a much smaller debt, and he didn't forgive him but abused him and threw him into prison. The violence and mistreatment of the second servant by the first servant was so appalling to the other servants that they reported it to the king, who was so angry (*orgizō*, v. 34) that he imprisoned the first servant.

In the parable of the great banquet (Mt 22:1-14), the king invited many guests to his son's wedding banquet. When the time came for the banquet, the potential guests not only neglected the invitation, making up excuses, but they also beat up and killed the king's messengers. The king was so enraged (*orgizō*) at the insult and the violent mistreatment of his servants that he retaliated by sending troops to destroy them.

While one needs to be careful about interpreting parables allegorically (where every aspect or character represents some thing or someone), in both of these parables the king clearly represents God. Jesus begins both by saying, "The kingdom of heaven may be compared to a king who . . ." (Mt 18:23; 22:2 ESV).

From these two parables of Jesus we can make three points about anger. First, the anger of the king is highlighted by Jesus. A parable reveals truth about God and God's kingdom, but it is still a made-up story. Jesus could construct these parables to make his point however he wanted, but he intentionally chose to portray the king—the God-character—as angry. Jesus is not embarrassed about God's emotions, particularly his anger. Jesus knows not only that God gets angry, but also that this truth about God needs to be revealed. Jesus told stories about an angry God because God is a God of wrath.

Second, the anger of the king is provoked when people are treated badly. The first parable makes the point that we should forgive, and the second makes the point that Jesus' followers need to prioritize God's kingdom; but in both the king only becomes angry when his servants are mistreated. Just as we saw in the Old Testament, these parables reveal a God that gets angry when people are oppressed. God's anger is motivated by his love.

Third, the anger of the king gets our attention. Not only does the God-character in these parables gets angry, in both cases the anger results in severe punishments. In the first parable, the servant who didn't forgive his fellow servant is handed over to be tortured. In the second, the king sent his soldiers to kill the people who murdered his servants. (And people say the God of Old Testament is the angry, violent one?) While the severity of the consequences suggests a connection to a final judgment, the tone of both still feels hyperbolic. We also need to remember these are fictional stories told by Jesus to make a point, and they aren't necessarily meant to be understood allegorically. The hyperbolic nature of the violence and anger get our attention, and they should make us heed the points Jesus is making about forgiveness and the priority of God's kingdom. Anger, it gets the job done.

"DON'T BE SO ANGRY!"

God gets angry, Jesus gets angry, but what about the people of God? I have a friend who is a youth pastor, and during the Black Lives Matter protests in the spring of 2020 she posted on social media about her frustration at the lack of response from White evangelicals to the Black Lives Matter movement. It was a reminder of what Martin Luther King Jr. said: "In the end, we will remember not the words of our enemies, but the silence of our friends."[17]

Many people from her church told her, "Don't be so angry on Facebook! God is in control." It's easy when you're not the victim of violence and oppression to say, "Don't be so angry." But sometimes we need to get angry. Paul lists anger as a work of the flesh (Gal 5:19-20), but he also says, "Be angry and do not sin" (Eph 4:26 ESV). Anger can be good or bad.

In his *Nicomachean Ethics*, Aristotle states, "Anyone can become angry—that is easy. But to be angry with the right person, to the right degree, at the right time, for the right purpose, and in the right way—that is not easy."[18] God's wrath is righteous—with the right person (the evildoer), to the right degree (seeking justice), at the right time (after a warning), for the right purpose (oppression), in the right way (slowly). Aristotle believes that anger should be used sparingly. I generally agree. But Aristotle's standard for appropriate anger may be too high and could prevent the people of God from being like God, who is after all a God of wrath. Scholar John Goldingay states, "The OT implies that anger along with (e.g.) hatred is a proper aspect of being a person. It has a place in the full-orbed character of God and thus in that of the human person made in God's image."[19]

The folks who told my friend "Don't be angry!" are followers of the Aristotelian School of Anger Management—only when everything is perfect do we get to display anger. But according to the Biblical School of Anger Management, it is appropriate to be angry when people are being oppressed, ideally when we're angry about oppression against others. When my friend told me about her experience, I said, "It sounds like your anger was righteous, like God's. More followers of Jesus need to express anger at injustice and oppression."

Moses was angry at the Israelites' construction of the golden calf (Ex 32:19). David was angry about the rich man who took, slaughtered, and cooked the poor man's precious lamb in Nathan's parable (2 Sam 12:5), but since David himself represented the rich man—he killed Uriah and took his wife (Bathsheba)—his anger was ultimately self-focused. Nehemiah was angry at his fellow Jews be-cause they were exploiting other Jews during the construction of the Jerusalem wall (Neh 5:6). In these incidents, these men of God were angry about the same things that prompted God's anger: idolatry (Moses), evil and violence (David), and oppression (Nehemiah). Anger is divine, but it should also be human. And therefore pastors, teachers, and church leaders need to talk more not only about God's anger, but how and when the people of God can and should be angry.

THE WRATH OF DAVE

Unlike God, Moses, David, and Nehemiah, the vast majority of times that I get angry, it's not righteous. Shortly after *God Behaving Badly* came out, New Testament scholar Scot McKnight posted a series of blogs on my book.[20] In response to Scot's fifth blog on the book (May 31, 2011) one of the commenters, Tom, advocated reading one of my chapters, then banging your head against the wall; he goes on, "Repeat until the sweet embrace of unconsciousness relieves your frustration." According to Tom, brain damage was preferable to reading my chapter.

I was furious about Tom's post. Utter humiliation on one of the biggest Christian blogs in the country. What made it particularly frustrating was that I had to prepare a talk later that afternoon, on anger, but I couldn't work because I was so mad and distracted. I started composing my response, "Hey Tom, when Scot McKnight posts a series of blogs on your book, then we'll talk. As if that would ever happen." Yeah, that's probably not what Jesus would have done. Fortunately, I refrained.

Then it felt like God spoke to me. "Dave, you're speaking later today on the topic of anger. Tom has just given you an example of unrighteous anger." I thought, "Wow. Thanks, Tom."

This was my reply: "Tom, sorry you didn't find the chapter helpful. Perhaps books by Chris Wright, Paul Copan, or Eric Seibert might do a better job for you. Thanks for your honesty." *That was hard to do.*

In the comments to Scot McKnight's sixth blog on the book, Tom apologized. We experienced blogosphere reconciliation. Sometimes anger is appropriate, but particularly when we feel we have been personally wronged Proverbs offers another alternative: "A soft answer turns away wrath" (Prov 15:1).

THE CUP OF WRATH

To find the ultimate expression of divine wrath and divine love together, we need to go to the New Testament. In Mark 14, when Jesus was in the Garden of Gethsemane shortly before he died, he prayed, "Abba, Father, for you all things are possible; remove this cup from me; yet, not what I want, but what you want" (Mk 14:36).

What cup is Jesus talking about? The cup of God's wrath. Passages from the prophetic books describe how the cup of God's wrath will be poured out upon people or nations for sin and disobedience (Is 51:17, 21-22; Jer 25:15; Lam 4:21; Ezek 23:32-34; Hab 2:16; Zech 12:2). That's the cup that Jesus knows he's supposed to drink, and, even though he is willing to submit to his Father, he understandably doesn't want his Father's anger to target him.

But what it meant for God to be a Father was that when his only begotten Son, whom he loved, said, "Dad, could you take that cup away?" God refused. Why? Love. God's anger over our sin was directed at Jesus on the cross. God so loved us, that he directed his wrath, not at me and you, but at his Son on the cross. As the father of two sons, I can't begin to comprehend this.

Jesus' actions here and throughout the Gospels serve as a reminder for any of us who wonder if God is angry at us—that the primary emotion God feels toward his people is not anger, but love. I am sometimes troubled by God's smiting anger. I am frequently motivated by God's righteous anger. But I am always amazed by God's abundant love.

4

the jealousy of god

The LORD, whose name is Jealous, is a jealous God.

EXODUS 34:14

AS I WAS WORKING ON THE TOPIC OF JEALOUSY, I encountered a quote attributed to Saint Augustine, "He who is not jealous does not love." To find the original source, I googled it. Fortunately, there were plenty of sites with the quote—it was deemed highly meme-worthy, with beautiful mountains and a setting sun.

However, as I reread Augustine's quote in its various internet manifestations, I noticed it was often missing the first not: "He who is jealous does not love." Huh? Apparently, Augustine now thinks jealousy is a bad thing. Many memes included an image of Augustine, but they all omitted the source. I assumed the North African church father didn't make completely contradictory statements in different contexts. Does Augustine think jealousy is good or bad?

To find a quote in the writings of Saint Mark you only have to read one work, his Gospel, sixteen chapters, 11,304 words (in Greek).[1] But Saint Augustine has over a hundred works totaling over five million words (in Latin),[2] so finding this jealousy quote would be like finding the proverbial needle in a haystack. I emailed the author of the article where I first encountered the Augustine quote.

Helpfully, he replied right away; unhelpfully, he didn't know the source either.

After spending several frustrating hours using high-powered library resources, I found an academic article that included the quote and, finally, provided the source, which I now share with you. I hope you're grateful.

> Now what expression, better than jealousy, can give us the idea of this feeling which exists in God insofar as he wants to contract with us the most real union, insofar as he forbids us to let ourselves be corrupted by a shameful love, which he pursues to revenge impurity, and surrounds the chastity of his love? Hence this adage full of truth: *He who is not jealous does not love.*[3]

The mystery was finally solved—Augustine thought jealousy was good. Interestingly, Augustine didn't come up with the line himself, but he was quoting a popular "adage full of truth." Unfortunately, he didn't include his source either (some things never change).

The context of the quote reveals why Augustine believes jealousy is good and an apt description of God. God intensely, jealously desires relationship with us. The version with the first "not" removed was more meme-worthy, but the double "not" version was more provocative and more profound.

Why was the first "not" removed? Apparently, jealousy is perceived so negatively that people couldn't imagine that Augustine would say something so positive about it. They either consciously or unconsciously changed the quote to fit what they think it should say. Augustine, however, thinks the jealousy of God is good. And as we'll see, God is often described as jealous. So, is jealousy good or bad? It depends.

THE JEALOUSY OF HERA, OTHELLO, AND THE KILLERS

In Greek mythology, divine jealousy was common, and bad. Because Zeus was often unfaithful, his wife Hera was often jealous.[4] While

Hera's jealousy was appropriate, how she chose to respond to it was not. Hera tried to kill Dionysus the son of Semele and Zeus, and she tormented Heracles the son of Alcemene and Zeus. Hera banned Leto (Zeus's lover) from giving birth on land. She turned Io (Zeus's lover) into a cow, and she turned Callisto (Zeus's lover) into a bear. Callisto's story has a happy ending since Zeus made her into a constellation, Ursa Major ("Big-She-Bear"), and it gets better for Callisto.[5] After their discovery by Galileo in the early 1600s, two of Jupiter's moons were named Io and Callisto. Since Jupiter is the Roman equivalent of the Greek god Zeus, Zeus's lovers got their revenge on Hera for her vengeful jealousy as they endlessly orbited around their big love planet.

About the time of Galileo, Shakespeare penned the play *Othello*, where Iago famously warns Othello, "Oh, beware, my lord, of jealousy! It is the green-eyed monster."[6] Jealousy is a monster, and yet it is one that Iago ironically wants to conjure since he secretly hopes Othello becomes jealous and kills his own wife. Iago is relying on the fact that jealousy is hard to resist for his plan to succeed.

More recently, the rock band The Killers' most popular single, "Mr. Brightside" (2003), tells of a man tormented by jealousy as his lover is with another man, "And I just can't look, it's killing me, and taking control . . . jealousy, turning saints into the sea."[7] In September 2020 the band performed "Mr. Brightside" from the rooftop of Caesars Palace during halftime for the Las Vegas Raiders first home game at Allegiant Stadium, broadcast on ESPN and ABC.[8] While many factors contribute to the popularity of a song (a great guitar riff), apparently millions of listeners felt a deep connection to the jealous emotions expressed in Mr. Brightside. From Greek mythology, Shakespeare, and The Killers, we see that jealousy is common, difficult to resist, and destructive to relationships. In these contexts, it's bad.

HEALTHY AND DESTRUCTIVE JEALOUSY

Jealousy can be good. If one's wife is spending too much time at work, healthy jealousy could prompt the husband to talk honestly about his feelings ("I'm jealous"), sharing why it's hard for him, because he misses her, and together they decide how to reprioritize work-family commitments.

However, jealousy can also be bad: when it stems from insecurity or anxiety, when it involves distrust or suspicion, when it leads to violent or abusive behavior. In those circumstances jealousy is obsessive and controlling. Unhealthy jealousy could cause a husband to become overprotective of his wife's friends of the opposite gender at work and can tragically lead to either verbal or physical abuse. Unhealthy jealousy is characterized by a lack of trust. Healthy jealousy is characterized by honest and gracious communication. When a spouse or a friend becomes obsessively jealous, most healthy individuals distance themselves. Unhealthy jealousy destroys relationships.

The reason the Augustine quote was often flipped is that many of us find it hard to conceive of contexts where jealousy is a good thing. And yet, jealousy has a legitimate place in healthy relationships. Psychology professor Noam Shpancer contrasts "reactive jealousy" which is generally healthy, with "suspicious jealousy" which is destructive. Shpancer explains how reactive jealousy is good. Reactive jealousy tends to be episodic in nature; it arises when a concrete outside threat to intimacy is introduced (someone is hitting on your guy). Reactive jealousy is mostly an emotional response to real, current outside threats and overt partner behaviors. The reactively jealous person is more conscious of their behavior, takes responsibility for it, and takes their partner's intent into account when evaluating the situation.[9]

Jealousy is a healthy emotion when connected to a real, not imaginary, threat and when the jealous partner is aware they are feeling it. As we examine God's jealousy in the Bible, we'll see how it generally meets these criteria for the healthy form of jealousy. To put it differently, jealousy is good when it honors the relationship. It realizes relationships are valuable, even precious. When threats arise to a relationship that is special or particularly valuable, they are taken seriously. Poet Maya Angelou captures the good and bad sides of jealousy well: "Jealousy in romance is like salt in food. A little can enhance the savor, but too much can spoil the pleasure and, under certain circumstances, can be life threatening."[10]

I don't think of myself as a jealous person, but I feel jealous sometimes about the travel schedule of my wife, Shannon. She travels to California multiple times a year to visit her recently widowed mother, twice a year to Liberia to assist the student Christian movement there, and many other times to various campus ministries on the East Coast. If I didn't miss her, it wouldn't bother me. But she's my best friend and I love being with her, so I'm jealous for her time when it seems like she's gone a lot. Sometimes my jealousy leads me to get bitter and make harsh comments, but that doesn't usually help and it certainly doesn't feel healthy. When I talk to her about it, I feel better, and she understands my perspective. Then we decide together on a travel schedule that takes seriously both the needs of her ministry and our marriage.

WORDS OF JEALOUSY

Unlike the many anger synonyms we saw in the last chapter, the Bible uses only a few words to describe divine jealousy, so table 4.1 of Hebrew and Greek words is short (the first two are Hebrew, the last two are Greek).[11]

Table 4.1. Jealousy in the Old and New Testament

Hebrew/ Greek	English	Divine jealous examples (ESV) (emphasis added)	Other references
qanna'	to be jealous	For I the LORD your God am a **jealous** God (Ex 20:5).	Ex 34:14; Deut 4:24; 5:9; 6:15
qin'ah	jealousy	I am exceedingly **jealous** for Jerusalem and for Zion (Zech 1:14).	Is 9:6; 37:32; 42:13; Ezek 5:13; 16:38

Hebrew/ Greek	English	Divine jealous examples (ESV) (emphasis added)	Other references
zēloō	to be jealous	Shall we provoke the Lord to **jealousy** (1 Cor 10:22)?	2 Cor 11:2
zēlos	jealousy	His disciples remembered that it was written, "**Zeal** for your house will consume me" (Jn 2:17).	2 Cor 11:2

In the Old Testament, the Hebrew verb *qanna'* and the related noun *qin'ah* can be translated as "to be jealous" or "jealousy" (Ex 20:5), but these terms can also be translated as "envy" (Gen 30:1; Ps 37:1) or "zeal" (2 Sam 21:2), depending on the context. Likewise, in the New Testament the Greek verb *zēloō* and the related noun *zēlos* have a similar semantic range, including "jealous(y)," "envy," or "zeal." Academic discussions often point out that these words can have either a positive or a negative connotation, depending on the context.[12]

Two examples from Paul's epistles to the Corinthians illustrate this tension. Paul tells the Corinthian church in his first epistle that "Love is ... not jealous" (*zēloō*; 1 Cor 13:4 NASB), which sounds a lot like the wrong Augustine quote, the one missing the first "not." But Paul declares to the Corinthians in his second epistle, "For I am jealous (*zēloō*) for you with a godly jealousy (*zēlos*)" (2 Cor 11:2). Thus, Paul links his own human jealousy for the Corinthians with God's jealousy for them as well. According to Paul, jealousy can be good or bad. In 2 Corinthians 11 Paul's godly jealousy is good because he wants his readers to be exclusively devoted to Christ. In 1 Corinthians 13, however, the jealousy is associated with boasting and arrogance, suggesting a suspicious jealousy focused on selfish desires—i.e., bad jealousy. Presumably, Paul is referring to bad jealousy when he speaks of it as a fruit of the flesh (Gal 5:20), in contrast to the fruit of the spirit, the first of which is love (Gal 5:22).

Since these words can sometimes, depending on the context, be translated as "envy" it might help to clarify the distinction. *Jealousy* (the healthy kind) involves a desire for something that is rightfully yours to have, like a wife has for her husband. *Envy*, however, involves a desire for something that is not yours to have, like a wife has for another woman's husband.[13]

"HE IS JEALOUS FOR ME"

Not all popular perceptions of jealousy are negative. Divine jealousy features prominently in the contemporary Christian song "How He Loves" by John Mark McMillan. The cover by David Crowder Band was nominated for a Dove Award for Rock/Contemporary Song of the Year in 2010.

> He is jealous for me,
> Loves like a hurricane . . .
> Oh how He loves us.[14]

McMillan's song describes reactive, healthy jealousy. God's intense love for his people may feel intense, hurricane-esque, but the author is overwhelmed by the beauty, affection, and love of God which moves him to sing. Divine jealousy is praiseworthy.

A JEALOUS GOD

When jealousy is associated with God in the Old Testament, it is portrayed positively. Let's begin our examination by looking at the Ten Commandments, the first instance jealousy is connected to God in the Bible.

> And God spoke all these words:
> "I am the LORD your God, who brought you out of Egypt, out of the land of slavery.
> "*You shall have no* other gods before me.
> "*You shall not make* for yourself an image in the form of anything in heaven above or on the earth beneath or in the waters below. *You shall not bow down* to them or [*you shall not*] *worship* them; for I, the LORD your God, am a **jealous God**, punishing

the children for the sin of the parents to the third and fourth generation of those who hate me, but showing love to a thousand generations of those who love me and keep my commandments." (Ex 20:1-6, emphasis added)

In the Reformed tradition these verses are considered the first two of the commandments, verse 3 is the first and verses 4-6 are the second. But in the Augustinian, Lutheran, and Catholic traditions, verses 3-6 are all part of the same first commandment, which makes more sense to me. The reason there are different numbering schemes among the various traditions is that the Ten Commandments include more than ten commands. I count fourteen commands in the Ten Commandments.[15]

I emphasized the four commands in four of these verses (vv. 3-6). Some English translations combine the third and fourth commands into one ("you shall not bow down or worship"), but in the Hebrew these phrases are more distinct, as I indicate with my parenthetical insertion. The commands forbidding having other gods (v. 3), making graven images (v. 4), and bowing down and worshiping graven images (v. 5) are all focused on one theme: idolatry. Thus, this first single commandment consists of four imperatives (having, making, bowing, worshiping) that call for one thing: exclusive devotion to God alone. Why? He is a jealous God. They are his people and he is their God; to display his commitment to them he just delivered his people from centuries of oppression by defeating the mighty nation of Egypt. That's better than roses and chocolates.

This description of God as jealous comes in the midst of this first commandment from the mouth of God himself. He has no qualms about declaring his jealousy for his people and for their exclusive worship. In the language of healthy, reactive jealousy, God is conscious of it and he takes responsibility for it. God agrees with Augustine (perhaps it's the other way around?); he thinks this type of jealousy is good.

A WILDERNESS WEDDING RING

After receiving the Ten Commandments (Ex 20) and the covenant code (Ex 21–23) on Mount Sinai, Moses returned to the people of Israel and together they established a covenant to obey all the commands God had just given them (Ex 24:1-8). A marriage ceremony is a familiar equivalent to this covenant ritual, where two parties vow to remain faithful, "To have and to hold, from this day forward . . ."

To help the Israelites remember their covenant with Yahweh, Moses took the blood from the oxen sacrifices, and splattered it on the people of Israel. As many of us are painfully aware, bloodstains are difficult to remove from one's clothes. It is likely that the Israelites had bloodstained covenant reminders—a bit like a wedding ring—on their garments for their forty-year wanderings in the wilderness.

When I teach on this covenant ceremony, I reenact it with the class. (Conveniently, there are several meat-packing plants nearby.) I use two squirter bottles filled with "blood" to spray my class, while we stand and vocally declare our allegiance to God. Before spraying, however, I inform the class that I'm using water for blood, but we still get wet. I hope the experience gives the students a taste of the visceral nature of the covenant described in the text, and ideally helps them remember their vows longer than the Israelites did.

ADULTERY ON THE HONEYMOON

Over the course of the next seven chapters (Ex 25–31) Moses received directions regarding the construction of the tabernacle and the ark, which served as a treasury for the precious covenant from God. The process took a while, so the people got restless and complained to Aaron, who constructed a golden calf for the people to worship (Ex 32:1-6). The scene then shifts from Aaron and the people, to Moses and Yahweh. In his anger, Yahweh commands Moses to leave, so his "wrath may burn hot" against the Israelites and consume them (Ex 32:10).

The people had just formalized their vows of faithfulness to God, and now they are worshiping an idol. The first commandment prohibited idolatry like the worship of this golden calf. To return to the marriage analogy, it is like the Israelites were committing adultery on the honeymoon.[16] And they were still wearing their "wedding clothes," their blood-stained covenant garments. Fortunately for Israel, Moses convinced Yahweh to change his mind about punishing his people who had broken covenant with him.[17]

Why was God so angry here? Jealousy. "He who is not jealous, does not love." In the aftermath of the incident of the golden calf, God renewed the covenant with his people. He not only reminded them he is a jealous God, but he declared his name is "Jealous" (Ex 34:14). One's name captured the essence of one's character. In Exodus 34:5-7, God is angry, compassionate, and loving, and in Exodus 34:14, he's jealous. Emotions are a fundamental, not peripheral, aspect of God's character.

According to Shpancer's definition, God's jealousy here is the healthy kind (reactive, not suspicious).[18] First, he is consciously aware of it—he mentions it at the beginning of the Ten Commandments and he reiterates it here after the golden calf. And second, his jealousy is provoked by a real threat—adultery on the honeymoon. Once again, God is not embarrassed about his emotions, but states quite boldly he is a jealous God. He values his relationship sufficiently so that he is willing to act in a manner to protect it.

"LET'S GO TO JAIL"

As I arrived home from California to visit my family in Iowa, my mom greeted me with, "Let's go to jail." Maybe I should have written home more often? Mom's exhortation actually wasn't prompted by a lack of correspondence but because she wanted to visit Ken, one of my younger brother's friends from high school, who was in prison.

The reason Ken was in jail was that he came home early from work one day to find his wife in bed with Brad, one of his best friends. Ken pulled out his shotgun and killed Brad. His jealousy was certainly reasonable. His response was clearly not. Whether we call it murder or justifiable homicide, his reaction was destructive, with tragic results for everyone involved.[19]

I wasn't comfortable with Mom's suggestion, so I started making excuses. Mom said, "Jesus told his followers that visiting people in prison was like visiting him" (Mt 25:36). I replied, "I haven't seen Ken in over seven years. He won't remember me." She persisted, "Let's go visit Jesus in prison." It's hard to say no to both Jesus and your mom. I finally agreed.

When we arrived at the jail any remaining hesitancy was quickly overcome with Ken's greeting: "Mrs. Lamb and David! It's so great to see you!" It was good we were there; God was clearly leading my mom to visit. Ken proceeded to tell us how God was working in his life. He had grown up going to church, but for the last ten years he hadn't felt the need or desire. But recent events and being in prison had awakened his sense of need for God. He was not only reading his Bible, but he was also leading two other inmates in a discussion of Matthew's Gospel. And he was able to be an encouragement to another inmate struggling with depression.

As we were leaving Ken gave us a poem he had written about his experience, which I saved. In it, he's a sparrow who is wounded and struggling, but finally hears a voice, "I, as the creator, have given you the strength to fly among the birds." God moves in mysterious ways. Despite the pain of this tragic incident prompted by jealousy, God somehow worked to call Ken back to himself.

WHERE ELSE IS GOD JEALOUS?

There are many passages in the Bible that describe God as jealous. I'll mention a few. God's repeated messages about his jealous nature were clearly received by the leaders of Israel and the authors of Scripture. In public speeches addressed to the entire nation, Moses and Joshua declare that God is a jealous God (Deut 4:24; 6:15; Josh 24:19). The psalmist speaks of God as jealous because of the idolatry of his people (Ps 78:58; 79:5). The prophets Joel, Nahum, and Zephaniah describe the intensity of God's jealousy (Joel 2:18; Nah 1:2; Zeph 1:18; 3:8). The prophet Ezekiel describes Yahweh as jealous six times in his book (Ezek 5:13; 16:42; 23:25; 36:5-6; 38;19; 39:25), while the prophet Zechariah uses forms of words for jealousy for Yahweh five times in just two verses (Zech 1:14; 8:2).[20]

In many of these passages, God's jealousy is connected to his wrath (Deut 29:20; 32:16, 21; Ps 78:58; 79:5; Nah 1:2; Zech 8:2). The book of Proverbs suggests that jealousy is a stronger emotion than anger, "Wrath is cruel, anger is overwhelming, but who can stand before jealousy?" (Prov 27:4). God is highly emotional—angry and jealous—and the text does not downplay this aspect of his character, but it also highlights and proclaims his emotional character throughout Scripture.

WHAT DOES DIVINE JEALOUSY ACCOMPLISH?

The phrase "For unto us a child is born" brings to mind for many of us images of Christmas, and perhaps specifically Handel's *Messiah*, but another association that should come to mind is divine jealousy. Long before Handel, the quotation originated from the prophet Isaiah.

> Nevertheless, there will be no more gloom for those who were in distress. In the past he humbled the land of Zebulun and the land of Naphtali, but in the future he will honor Galilee of the nations, by the Way of the Sea, beyond the Jordan—
> The people walking in darkness have seen a great light;
> on those living in the land of deep darkness a light has dawned.
> You have enlarged the nation and increased their joy;

they rejoice before you as people rejoice at the harvest,

as warriors rejoice when dividing the plunder.

For as in the day of Midian's defeat,

you have shattered the yoke that burdens them,

the bar across their shoulders, the rod of their oppressor.

Every warrior's boot used in battle and every garment rolled in
    blood

will be destined for burning, will be fuel for the fire.

For to us a child is born, to us a son is given,

and the government will be on his shoulders.

And he will be called Wonderful Counselor, Mighty God,
    Everlasting Father, Prince of Peace.

Of the greatness of his government and peace there will be no end.

He will reign on David's throne and over his kingdom,

establishing and upholding it with justice and righteousness

from that time on and forever.

The **zeal** (*qin'ah*) of the LORD Almighty will accomplish this.

(Is 9:1-7, emphasis added)

These seven verses are full of emotions. To those who had experienced gloom and distress (v. 1), Yahweh will give joy and rejoicing (v. 3). The prophecy elaborates the source of the joy as those walking in darkness will be shown a great light (v. 2) when Yahweh defeats their enemies (vv. 3-5). And all of these things will be accomplished because of God's zeal (v. 7).

This emotionally rich text also includes a dramatic prediction with messianic implications. The child who is born, the Son who is given will be called "Wonderful Counselor, Mighty God, Everlasting Father, Prince of Peace" (9:6). The great kingdom of this Davidic ruler will be characterized by peace, justice, and righteousness (9:7).

While many of us may be familiar with this text, having heard, perhaps even preached, sermons on it during Advent, the curious ending is often ignored. The passage concludes by providing an explanation for how all this happened: "The zeal (*qin'ah*) of Yahweh Almighty will accomplish this" (v. 7). There are several observations we can make about this zeal.

All these amazing things listed in this prophecy happened because God's zeal accomplished it. The emotions of God were not merely felt. The impact of God's zeal are described as wonderful, mighty, everlasting, and great. The kingdom that is established as a result of God's zeal is majestic, peaceful, just, and righteous. Isaiah does not ignore, or downplay God's emotion here, but he highlights it by first describing its wondrous impact and then concluding this passage by dramatically revealing its cause—divine zeal.

While we might expect God's love would be the cause, it is his zeal that served as the catalyst for these amazing and glorious acts. The word translated into "zeal" is *qin'ah*, which, as we've already seen, is most frequently translated as "jealousy." The emotion expressed here is similar in many respects to jealousy, which is why several scholars speak of jealousy in their discussions of this text.[21] Zeal is intensely passionate. It is focused on God's concern for his relationship with his people, and it is expressed in response to a threat as the people of God have greatly suffered from their enemies. The New Living Translation renders *qin'ah* here as "passionate commitment," which sounds like healthy, reactive jealousy.

God's zeal, or jealousy, somehow contributed to the most significant act of divine love, God sending his Son as Messianic Savior. The promised Counselor-God-Father-Prince child is coming because of the jealousy of God.

How does this passage actually connect to Jesus? We must acknowledge that poetic texts are difficult to fully comprehend, and that the message presumably had an initial fulfillment during the life of Isaiah, otherwise it wasn't good news for the people of his day ("In 700 years good things will happen, so cheer up!"). But this text has three points of connection to Jesus via Matthew's Gospel. First, the messianic ruler will be Davidic (Is 9:7), and as Matthew's genealogy informs us, Jesus was not only the Messiah, the Christ, he was also a descendant of David (Mt 1:1). Second, the birth of the child of Isaiah 9 can be linked to the birth of the Immanuel child of Isaiah 7, which Matthew also connects to Jesus (Mt 1:22-23). Third, Matthew connects this passage directly to Jesus by quoting Isaiah 9:1-2 to explain how Jesus' ministry in Galilee fulfills the words of Isaiah (Mt 4:13-16). According to Isaiah and Matthew, the emotions of God, specifically his jealous zeal, played a key role in God sending Jesus into the world as Prince of Peace.

HUMANS JEALOUS FOR GOD

Some particularly troubling biblical stories involve humans acting jealously for God when the Israelites were involved in idolatry.[22] Phinehas, the grandson of Aaron, speared an Israelite man and a Midianite woman while they were having sex and thus his jealousy prevented more Israelites from dying by plague (both *qanna'* and *qin'ah* appear in Num 25:11, 13). Sexual relations between Israelites and Midianites were connected to worship of their god, Baal of Peor. The prophet Elijah twice declared that he was jealous for Yahweh while the Israelites were unfaithful to the covenant and killing Yahweh's prophets (*qanna'* appears four times in 1 Kings 19:10, 14). Elijah's interaction with Yahweh took place after he slaughtered all the prophets of Baal after defeating them on Mount Carmel. King Jehu of Israel told his friend Jehonadab to witness his zeal (*qin'ah*) for Yahweh in the midst of his slaughters of the household of idolatrous King Ahab and the worshipers of Baal (2 Kings 10:16). Disturbingly, in each of these incidents of human jealousy, severe violence was involved.

While it is difficult to fully comprehend the violence of these troubling acts of bloodshed, three points may help us make more sense of it.[23] First, while God seems either to affirm or to not comment on these violent acts afterward, in none of these instances does God command them beforehand. And the book of Hosea makes it clear that Jehu's zealous violence went too far, "I will punish the house of Jehu for the blood of Jezreel" (Hos 1:4 ESV).

Second, the violent acts performed by Phinehas, Elijah, and Jehu could easily have prevented even greater bloodshed. Yahweh says Phinehas' zeal stopped the plague (Num 24:11). Speaking more generally, Yahweh blessed the nation when they were faithful to the covenant (Deut 28:1-14), but when they worshiped other gods, his protection was removed and they were taken over by their enemies (Deut 28:15-68).

Third, the violence in these contexts was not an innovation of Phinehas, Elijah, and Jehu. The Israelites in the wilderness had just been attacked by the Moabites and the Ammonites, and would go to war against Midian a few chapters later. Yahweh's prophets were being slaughtered en mass by Ahab and his queen Jezebel, and Jezebel had just ordered a "hit" on Elijah. Jehu had been the commander of Israel's army, and before, during, and after his reign the Israelites were constantly battling the Arameans. One could say, these texts fit into the context of world of "an eye for an eye" (Lev 24:19-20). The trajectory of God's Word in both the Old and New Testament on the subject of violence is away from "eye for an eye" toward loving our enemies (1 Sam 24:3-7; 2 Kings 6:21-23; Prov 25:21; Is 2:4; Jer 29:7; Mic 4:3; Mt 5:39, 44; Lk 9:54-56).

While the violence of these stories is still troubling, the takeaway for this chapter is that each of these individuals were jealous for God. They were portrayed positively not for their violence, but for their jealous—first commandment-esque—zeal for God, that the nation of Israel would worship not idols, but God alone, an attitude we find also in Jesus.

THE ZEAL OF JESUS

Jesus frequently expressed emotions, and perhaps his most dramatic outburst of emotion involved his cleansing of the temple. In John's version of the event, the disciples interpret his actions as zeal.

> When it was almost time for the Jewish Passover, Jesus went up to Jerusalem. In the temple courts he (Jesus) found people selling cattle, sheep and doves, and others sitting at tables exchanging money. So he made a whip out of cords, and drove all from the temple courts, both sheep and cattle; he scattered the coins of the money changers and overturned their tables. To those who sold doves he said, "Get these out of here! Stop turning my Father's house into a market!" His disciples remembered that it is written: "Zeal (*zēlos*) for your house will consume me." (Jn 2:13-17)

What makes Jesus so upset? In a word, idolatry. People here are worshiping money (selling, exchanging money, making the temple into a market), and not worshiping God in God's house. In the place where people should be praying and praising, they are selling and buying.

The Greek word for zeal here is *zēlos* which, as noted above, is often translated as "jealousy" (e.g., Acts 5:17; Rom 13:13; Jas 3:16). The quotation comes from Psalm 69, "For zeal (*qin'ah*) for your house consumes me" (Ps 69:9). Psalm 69 is distinctive among the Psalms for two reasons. It is one of the most emotional psalms, and one of the most frequently quoted by the New Testament. The Hebrew word for zeal in Psalm 69 is *qin'ah*, which is typically translated as jealousy (e.g., Prov 27:4; Ps 79:5; Zech 1:14). Thus, the semantic range of both the Hebrew and Greek words for this text includes jealousy. John sets this story immediately following a wedding (Jn 2:1-11), an image of covenant fidelity, and now Jesus is upset about idolatry taking place in his "father's house." As we saw in Exodus, from the perspective of a covenant relationship with God, idolatry is like adultery. Jesus' response in John 2 looks like jealousy.

We can make three more observations about Jesus' zeal here. First, Jesus' zeal was dramatic. Emotions are not merely felt, but for Jesus they led to violent behavior (making a whip, scattering coins, overturning tables). Second, Jesus' zeal was memorable. The disciples reflected on it later, presumably after his death, and his zealous actions led them to recall Psalm 69. Dramatic and memorable. While my wife, Shannon, was leading a Bible study of Jesus' cleansing of the temple in Mark (11:15-17) she actually flipped over a table with books, pens, cups, and papers. Everyone was shocked, but they will never forget it. Third, Jesus' zeal was consuming. The emotional response Jesus felt when confronted with massive idolatry was overwhelming. In John's Gospel, this was Jesus' first confrontation with the religious leaders. His consuming zeal/jealousy served as a catalyst for their campaign of persecution that led to his crucifixion, just as Jesus had predicted, "Destroy this temple, and in three days I will raise it up" (Jn 2:19 ESV).

OUR JEALOUS GOD

While jealousy is often unhealthy, hopefully we've also seen that it can be a good thing, and that God's jealousy for us is healthy, even praiseworthy. How can we respond to this realization? I see three ways. First, know that God's love for us is jealous and that he desires our exclusive focus. Just as a husband can bask in the knowledge that his wife loves him uniquely, so can the people of God delight knowing that our God is a jealous God, and that we are the objects of his love. We should read our Bibles in light of this truth.

Second, tell the people who you are most likely to feel jealous toward how and why you value your relationship with them. For most of us, these will be our closest family members (spouses, children, parents, or siblings). Healthy relationships are honest relationships. We can learn from God's example about being honest about our healthy jealousy toward the people we love.

Third, because God desires that all people are in an exclusive relationship with him, tell people that God jealously loves them. Anything other than God that we devote our lives to will ultimately not satisfy our needs or wants. Only God can do that, which is why he loves us jealously.

AUGUSTINE'S CONFESSION

Saint Augustine was not afraid of honest expressions of emotion, as evidenced in what has been called the greatest spiritual autobiography of all time, his *Confessions*. When he was young, Augustine rejected the Christianity of his mother, Monica, and became a professor of philosophy and rhetoric. While talking with friends one day, he heard about the dramatic conversion of two wealthy men who read about the life of Saint Anthony and decided to live as monks.[24] He said he loved these men who he was hearing about and began to hate himself for his various desires that prevented him from following their path.[25]

The story was deeply troubling to Augustine as he reflected on his various idols. He described his "zeal for wisdom" and his struggles with lust. When he was young he had prayed, "Give me chastity . . . but not yet."[26] He was afraid God would heal him quickly "of that disease of lust." He continues to describe his internal struggles, with his friend Alypius "standing close by my side, silently awaited the outcome of my strange emotion."[27] He wept, "the floods burst from my eyes," as he prayed: "How long, O Lord, will you be angry forever?"[28] The verse that Augustine quotes here comes from Psalm 79:5, and it continues, "Will your jealousy burn like fire?" Augustine was familiar with divine jealousy.

In the midst of his turmoil, Augustine heard a small voice, like that of a child, "Take up, and read. Take up and read." At first he thought nearby children were playing a game, but then he realized God was speaking to him. He remembered how God had spoken to Saint Anthony as he heard a reading of Jesus' words to the rich young man, "Go, sell what you have, and give to the poor, and you shall have treasure in heaven, and come, follow me" (Mt 19:21).[29] So he went to where his friend Alypius was standing and picked up a copy of Paul's letters. He opened it randomly and read from Romans, "Not in orgies and drunkenness, not in sexual immorality and sensuality, not in quarreling and jealousy. But put on the Lord Jesus Christ, and make no provision for the flesh, to gratify its desires" (Rom 13:13-14 ESV).

He told Alypius what had happened. Alypius read the next verse, "As for the one who is weak in faith, welcome him" (Rom 14:1 ESV), which he assumed applied to him. The two of them decided to undertake an ascetic lifestyle ("I would seek neither wife nor ambition in this world").[30] The jealous love of God had finally broken through to them. God had convicted Augustine about his idolatries of sex, wisdom, and money, and his need to be jealously committed to Jesus. When Augustine shared the news with his mother, she rejoiced as confessed by her son, "You turned her mourning into a joy." Augustine spent the next four decades serving God first as a priest, then a bishop, writing over five million words (in Latin), including "He who is not jealous, does not love."

5

the sorrow of god

Jesus wept.

JOHN 11:35

SHANNON AND I WERE AT THE FINAL DINNER of a two-day board meeting for my seminary which included a celebration to honor our theology professor, Todd Mangum, who had recently been promoted to full professor. I was going to make a few comments to praise and roast my colleague and friend. Right as I was about to share my remarks, I received a phone call from my brother-in-law Randall's ex-wife. I was tempted to not answer it because of the timing, but I figured it must be important since she rarely called me. "Hi, Dave, I've got some very bad news. Randall died this morning." My heart sank. "Oh, no!"

After hanging up, I turned to Shannon, who was sitting next to me, "That was Tracy. Your brother passed away this morning." We were in shock. He was only forty-seven years old. But as is often the case in these types of situations, we had no time to grieve. We needed to think about logistics. Do Shannon's parents know about the fate of their son yet? (They didn't.) Do we tell people around our table, or just make a hasty exit? (We told them.) How should we inform our two boys that their uncle was gone? (We told them in person when we got home.)

As we were leaving, Todd's father, Glenn, who was present for the dinner to honor his son, said, "Wait! Come, let's pray." He was also a retired pastor. He called a few of our friends to gather around us. Glenn prayed that we would somehow experience the grace and comfort of God in the midst of this terrible loss. The time of prayer finally provided a chance to slow down and grieve. We wept.

Even though the Gospels only record two instances, Jesus probably wept on many occasions (despite what "Away in the Manger" might suggest). Perhaps the most familiar time is when Lazarus, the brother of his close friends Mary and Martha, died. As we prayed with Pastor Glenn and our friends, the knowledge that our Savior weeps alongside people who have lost brothers was a great comfort to us. The sorrow of God, perhaps more than any other divine emotion, provides those of us in pain with a safe place to grieve, mourn, and weep.

DEFINING SORROW

Sorrow is a feeling, an emotional response caused by a negative circumstance: pain, sin, oppression, death. Things are not as they should be, prompting sadness. The bad things are happening, either to the one feeling the sorrow, or to others whom the sorrowful person cares about. In Plutchik's wheel of emotions, in order of increasing intensity, pensiveness becomes sadness, which becomes grief. In this chapter, we will see that the God of both testaments often expresses sorrow. In the Gospels, Jesus wept; in the Prophets, Yahweh wept. As we examine divine sorrow, we will discover profound lessons about God, his character, and what it means to be the people of God.

WORDS OF SORROW

A short discussion of a few of the Hebrew and Greek words the Bible uses to describe sorrow will help us understand how these terms are used. I've constructed two tables of terms, table 5.1 for the Old Testament (Hebrew) and table 5.2 for the New Testament (Greek).

Table 5.1. Sorrow in the Old Testament

Hebrew	English	Divine sorrow examples (NRSV) (emphasis added)	Other references
naham	was sorry	And the LORD was **sorry** that he had made humankind on the earth (Gen 6:6a).	Judg 2:18; 1 Sam 15:11, 35
'atsav	grieve	And it **grieved** him to his heart (Gen 6:6b).	Ps 78:40; Is 63:10
bakah	weep	Therefore I **weep** with the weeping of Jazer for the vines of Sibman (Is 16:9).	Jer 9:10; 48:32
beki	weeping	More than for Jazer I **weep** for you, O vine of Sibmah (Jer 48:32).	Is 16:9

The Hebrew verb *naham* can mean "was sorry" (Gen 6:6-7) or "regret" (1 Sam 15:11, 35. *Naham* can also mean "moved to pity," Judg 2:18, which will be discussed in chapter 8). The Hebrew verb *'atsav* can refer to physical pain, to hurt (Eccles 10:9), but it usually refers to emotional sorrow, to "grieve" (Gen 6:6; Ps 78:40; Is 63:10). The verb *bakah*, "weep," is used frequently (115 times in the Old Testament), primarily with human subjects (Gen 21:16; 37:35), but also occasionally for God (Is 16:9; Jer 9:10; 48:32). Three instances where *bakah* involves weeping for joy (Gen 29:11; 33:4; 46:29) will be discussed in chapter six. The related noun *beki*, "weeping," is used mainly of humans (Gen 45:2; Judg 21:2), but it is also used for God (Is 16:9; Jer 48:32). In at least one instance, each of these Hebrew terms for sorrow are associated with God.

Table 5.2. Sorrow in the New Testament

Greek	English	Divine sorrow examples (ESV) (emphasis added)	Other references
lypeō	grieve	And taking with him Peter and the two sons of Zebedee, he began to be **sorrowful** and troubled (Mt 26:37).	2 Cor 7:9, 11; Eph 4:30
klaiō	weep	When he drew near and saw the city, he **wept** over it (Lk 19:41).	Rom 12:15
dakryō	weep	Jesus **wept** (Jn 11:35).	

Greek	English	Divine sorrow examples (ESV) (emphasis added)	Other references
dakryon	weeping	Jesus offered up prayers and supplications, with loud cries and **tears** (Heb 5:7).	Lk 7:44; Acts 20:31

Shifting to the New Testament, the Greek verb *lypeō* means "grieve," "be sad," or "be sorrowful" and it appears twenty-six times (Mt 26:37; 2 Cor 7:9, 11; Eph 4:30). Two other related forms of *lypeō* will be mentioned within their contexts below, the adjective *perilypos* (Mt 26:38; Lk 18:24) and the verb *syllypeō* (Mk 3:5). The Greek verb *klaiō*, "weep," (Jn 11:33) is used forty times in the New Testament, often signifying a strong emotion (Phil 3:18), and involving loud wailing (Mt 2:18; Rev 18:9), including once for Jesus (Lk 19:41—see below). The verb *dakryō*, "weep," only appears once in the New Testament, in the shortest verse of the Bible when Jesus wept (Jn 11:35). The related noun *dakryon*, "weeping," is used in Hebrews to describe Jesus' tears while he prayed (Heb 5:7). Thus, we see that a variety of terms are used to describe the sorrow of Yahweh in the Old Testament and of Jesus in the New.

A TIME TO WEEP AND MOURN

In the context of divine hate in chapter two we looked at how the "a time for everything" poem of Ecclesiastes 3 counsels readers about the timely appropriateness of various experiences. The poem pairs opposites: birth and death, silence and speaking, love and hate, war and peace. In verse 4, weeping is paired with laughing, and mourning with dancing.

> A time to weep (*bakah*) and a time to laugh,
> a time to mourn (*saphod*) and a time to dance. (Eccles 3:4)

On Robert Plutchik's wheel, sadness is the opposite of joy, and the Ecclesiastes poem seems to agree. But the poem also suggests a movement, or a natural progression from sorrow to joy, as weeping becomes laughing and mourning becomes dancing. It is not unusual for a cathartic cry to lead to a welcome laugh, which is why this deep dive into sorrow will be followed in the next chapter by an examination of joy.

GOD PROCESSED HIS SORROW

Curiously, in the first few chapters of Genesis there is no explicit reference to a divine emotional response, even in places we might expect it: the eating of the fruit (3:6), the birth of the children of Adam and Eve (4:1-2), or the murder of Abel by his brother Cain (4:8).[1] The first explicit display of divine emotion in Scripture is sorrow in response to human wickedness and violence right before the flood.[2]

> The LORD saw that the wickedness of humankind was great in the earth, and that every inclination of the thoughts of their hearts was only evil continually. And the LORD **was sorry** (*naham*) that he had made humankind on the earth, and it **grieved** (*'atsav*) him to his heart. So the LORD said, "I will blot out from the earth the human beings I have created—people together with animals and creeping things and birds of the air, for I **am sorry** (*naham*) that I have made them." But Noah found favor in the sight of the LORD. (Gen 6:5-8 NRSV, emphasis added)

An English translation of the Septuagint (the early Greek translation of the Hebrew Bible, finished several centuries before Christ) of Genesis 6:6 is rendered thus, "Then God laid it to heart that he had made man upon the earth, and he pondered *it* deeply" (Gen 6:6). Even though the original Hebrew words clearly denote strong emotion, in the Septuagint God isn't sorry or grieved, but concerned and pondering. Thus, it appears that the tradition of suppressing divine emotions goes back well before the time of Jesus.

In Genesis 6, God is sorry (*naham*) that he had made the humans. The text emphasizes God's emotions here by twice stating he was sorry (vv. 6-7), and once stating he was grieved to his heart (v. 6), three repetitions of divine sorrow in two verses. The text puts two of these descriptions in the voice of the narrator, and strikingly once in the voice of God himself. While humans often hide or cover up emotions like grief or sorrow, here neither the narrator nor God himself were embarrassed about divine expressions of emotion.

Two questions often arise when I teach this text. First, *Who is God talking to?* It appears that he is talking to himself. I would say God processes his emotions by verbalizing them, which is generally a healthy way to respond to a tragic situation. When we ignore or downplay divine emotions, we are essentially repressing experiences that the biblical text has recorded for us to grapple with (see Paul's words on this in Romans 15:4). And as we reflect on how God experiences and expresses his emotions, we learn appropriate ways to deal with suffering and sorrow. While many of us struggle to talk about our griefs and sorrows, God here models a healthy alternative.

The second question is, *How could an omniscient God regret doing anything?* I understand why people ask this question, but intriguingly the text here has no interest in answering, or even addressing it. This passage is not concerned with divine omniscience, but with divine emotions. Genesis 6 emphasizes that God is emotional, specifically, that he is grieved.

However, the text is concerned with the question, *why* is God sorrowful here? This passage makes it clear that human sin caused the divine sorrow. When God saw the sin of the people of Noah's day, he was sorrowful and grieved. Specifically, a few verses after this section, the wickedness is clarified as human bloodshed, "The earth was filled with violence" (Gen 6:11, 13). After the flood, God states that if someone kills another human they deserve to die, because humans are made in the image of God (Gen 9:6). God was grieved because his freshly created, divine image-bearers were killing each other.

Parents watching their children fight might relate to how God felt in Genesis 6. On those rare instances when our two young sons fought and hurt each other (as siblings do) it was excruciating for my wife and me, since we so desperately wanted them to not only get along but to love each other. I assume my parents felt similarly with me. There was the time when I was five and I was frustrated with my cousin, so I smashed a lawn chair on his head, knocking him unconscious. Or when I was eight and was so mad at my older brother that I picked up a desk chair and smashed a hole in his bedroom door. They decided to never repair the door, which served as a reminder of my out-of-control violent behavior. (I've now gone over fifty years without committing an act of violence with a chair. I'm sure my parents would be proud.)

As we saw in chapters two, three, and four, human sin may cause God to hate (Ps 5:5), to be angry (Judg 2:12), or to be jealous (Ex 20:5). But as the biblical narrative is laid out, before sin prompted God to display any of these other emotions, it prompted him first to be profoundly sorrowful. It is good that the pervasiveness of violence against humans affected God emotionally, making him sorrowful, and grieving him to his heart. It is easy for us to become desensitized to human suffering and violence. However, as our examination of divine sorrow will reveal, the God of the Bible remains softhearted, grieved by harm done to humans created in his image. As the creator of all emotions, God feels intense sorrow, much more so than humans do. Based on Genesis 6 and other texts like it, we can be confident that our God continues to feel grief, sorrow, and sadness over how humans treat each other today.

GOD REGRETTED

Shortly after the parting of the Red Sea, as the Israelites were leaving Egypt, they were attacked by the Amalekites (Ex 17:8-16). Israel had no military training or experience, but God led them to victory over the Amalekites (only while Moses' tired arms were supported by Aaron and Hur). Centuries later when Saul became king, Yahweh spoke to Saul via the prophet Samuel, and told him to wipe out the Amalekites because they attacked Israel while they were tired and faint (1 Sam 15:1-3). Most problematically from a moral standpoint, the Amalekites specifically targeted the weak (Deut 25:17-19). Biblical scholar Christopher Wright describes the probable victims of the Amalekite attack described in Deuteronomy 25, "Those lagging behind would have been the elderly, and the very young, the sick, pregnant women, etc."[3] Saul obeyed the part of the commission about killing the Amalekites, but didn't kill their animals or their king, Agag (1 Sam 15:4-9). I discuss the problem of a violent God who appears to command genocide elsewhere,[4] so here I'll focus on the problem of an emotional God who regrets his choice of a king.

God processes his emotions with Samuel, who played a major role in making Saul king earlier (1 Sam 8 12). God laments with his prophet, "I regret (*naham*) that I have made Saul king, because he has turned away from me and has not carried out my instructions" (1 Sam 15:11). Commentators point out the similarities between 1 Samuel 15 and Genesis 6; human sin prompts divine sorrow prior to judgment.[5] Perhaps most striking is the use of the verb *naham* in both texts, translated variously as "regret"[6] or "be sorry."[7] The narrative also concludes with a similar observation, not from Yahweh's voice, but from the narrator, using the same verb (*naham*) describing God's sorrow over Saul's behavior (1 Sam 15:11, 35). This bookending comment serves to emphasize the importance of divine grief in this story. Once again, the biblical text doesn't hide God's emotions, but highlights them with repetition and prominent location.

Why did Yahweh regret here? He doesn't regret that Amalekites need to be punished, but that he made Saul king. Saul's inability to follow orders is interpreted by Yahweh here as a turning away from Yahweh (1 Sam 15:11). It wasn't merely disobedience, but a rejection of Yahweh, which explains why Yahweh would have an emotional response to it. Once again, human action prompted divine emotion, in this case sorrow.

GOD WAS BROKEN, HURT, GRIEVED, CRUSHED, AND ANGUISHED

Consistently, the catalyst for divine sorrow throughout the Old Testament is human sin. The disobedience in the wilderness is framed as rebellion against God, which prompted God to grieve (Ps 78:40). Similar language is used in Isaiah to describe Israel's generalized rebellion which caused God's Spirit to grieve (Is 63:10). John Goldingay states, "Relating to us involves Yhwh in sorrow and sadness," then he lists dozens of other Old Testament texts which describe divine sadness, letdown, and grief (Is 1:2-3; 5:2-7; 48:18; 49:4; 53:4; Jer 2:1-8; 3:19-20; Hos 6:4; 11:7).[8] In the book of Ezekiel, Yahweh declares, "I have been broken over their whoring heart that has departed from me and over their eyes that go whoring after their idols" (Ezek 6:9 ESV). The difficulty of comprehending the intensity of God's emotions in Ezekiel 6:9 is evidenced by the variety of terms used by English translations to describe it, as God is "broken" (ESV, KJV), "hurt" (NASB, NLT), "grieved" (NIV), "crushed" (NRSV), "anguished" (JPS). God is not detached or indifferent to the fate of humanity. Human sin and rebellion affect God emotionally, causing grief, regret, and sorrow to the point where he is broken, crushed, and anguished.

GOD WEPT

Isaiah 15–16 includes an oracle concerning the destruction of Moab, one of Israel's neighbors to the southeast (see Gen 19:30-38). Most likely, the devastation this oracle describes occurred at the hands of the Assyrians under either Sargon II or Sennacherib (roughly 720–700 BC). We can discern three distinct voices in this oracle, the Moabites, the prophet Isaiah, and God himself. I will focus just on the verses where God is speaking about his emotions. His emotional reaction here is shocking.

> **My heart cries out** for Moab; his fugitives flee to Zoar . . .
> Therefore I **weep** (*bakah*) with the **weeping** (*beki*) of Jazer for
> the vines of Sibmah;
> I drench you with **my tears**, O Heshbon and Elealeh;
> for the shout over your fruit harvest and your grain harvest
> has ceased . . .
> Therefore **my heart throbs** like a harp for Moab. (Is 15:5; 16:9,
> 11 NRSV, emphasis added)

Before examining the emotions expressed, we need to make two clarifying comments. First, all of the locations mentioned in these verses are Moabite (Zoar, Jazer, Sibmah, Heshbon, Elealeh—it's okay if you didn't know where these were, I didn't either). Second, the context makes it clear that Yahweh is the one speaking about his emotions. He states that he is the one causing the judgment (Is 15:9; 16:10), and the oracle concludes, "This is the word that the LORD spoke concerning Moab" (Is 16:14 NRSV).[9]

Even as he inflicts the punishment, God weeps alongside the residents of Moab. The heart of God cries out in pain; it throbs like a harp. Perhaps the best image for divine tears would be a tsunami, which in this case drenched the people of Moab. God's throbbing heart, his cries, and his tears were all demonstrations of his intense sorrow over the sin and subsequent judgment that came upon Moab. Biblical scholar Alec Motyer summarizes the passionate emotions of God here, "The divine nature expressed itself in wrath; but there is another side to the Lord, a heart of astonishing sympathy and empathy, compassion and identification with human suffering."[10] While the world we live in is full of schadenfreude—finding joy in the suffering of our enemies—the God who created the world finds no joy in the pain of others, but rather he suffers alongside humans who suffer.

The book of Jeremiah includes a similar divine lament where God again weeps and wails over Moab (Jer 48:30-32). And in Jeremiah 9, God declares that he will weep and wail for his creation—mountains, pastures, cattle, birds, and animals—because of the destruction coming upon Jerusalem and Judah (Jer 9:10-11).[11] The tragedy of the pain felt by his people, by their neighbors, and by his creation had a dramatic effect on our emotional God. He wept.

"THIS WILL HURT ME MORE THAN IT WILL HURT YOU"

When I was young and did something really bad (i.e., vandalized doors, hit my cousin on the head with a lawn chair, threw snowballs at cars, climbed on the roof at school) my father spanked me. I don't recommend this behavior, but it made an impression on me. I wasn't spanked often, but each time I vividly remember my father saying, "This will hurt me more than it hurts you." I would reply, "Let's switch places then!" My counterproposal was always rejected.

Obviously, the emotional pain my father felt was different from the physical pain I felt during these times of punishment, and there is no way to subjectively evaluate which would hurt more. Now that I am a parent, I can better appreciate his words, as well as God's words in the oracles over Moab and his lament for creation (Is 15–16; Jer 9; 48), as he described his anguished cries, his weeping, his tears. It is more difficult to punish when you truly love someone. Once again, we see human sin prompts a sentence of divine judgment, but even as God is meting out the righteous punishment, he weeps for the people and animals he loves.

THE BIBLE IS FULL OF WEEPERS

There are too many instances of the people of God expressing sorrow throughout Scripture, so I will focus on examples of weeping since it is a clear, tangible, and dramatic expression of sorrow. The Bible is full of weepers. And it clearly views this behavior positively. Abraham wept at the death of Sarah (Gen 23:2). The Bible records Joseph weeping at least seven times. He wept after overhearing his old brother Reuben rebuke his other brothers for harming Joseph decades earlier (Gen 42:24). He wept when he first saw his full-brother Benjamin and then again later when he was reunited with Benjamin and his other brothers (Gen 43:30; 45:14-15). He wept when he was reunited with his father Jacob, and when his father died (Gen 46:29; 50:1). He wept when his brothers asked for forgiveness vicariously through the voice of their deceased father (Gen 50:17).

Unlike the little Lord Jesus in the Christmas carol, baby Moses cried. It was the first thing he did (Ex 2:6). Hannah wept while she prayed for a son. God heard her prayer and she gave birth to Samuel, the great prophet (1 Sam 1:10). Like Joseph, King David had a rough life; and like Joseph, David wept a lot, at least seven times (1 Sam 30:4; 2 Sam 1:11-12; 3:32; 12:21-22; 13:36; 15:30; 18:33). The prophet Elisha wept as he foresaw the evil fate future King Hazael of Aram would inflict upon Israel (2 Kings 8:11-12). God mentioned not only Hezekiah's prayer, but also his tears as he changed his mind and gave Hezekiah fifteen more years of life (2 Kings 20:3-5).[12] Righteous King Josiah humbled himself and wept, so the prophetess Huldah pronounced that God would show him mercy (2 Kings 22:18-20). For good reason Jeremiah is called the weeping prophet, and he declared, "Oh that my head were waters, and my eyes a fountain of tears, that I might weep day and night for the slain of the daughter of my people" (Jer 9:1; Mt 8:23). Queen Esther wept and pleaded with King Ahasuerus of Persia for the lives of the Jews (Esther 8:3). Ezra the priest led the nation in a time of confession and weeping over the ways they had disobeyed God in marrying non-Israelites (Ezra 10:1).

There's more in the New Testament. Peter wept after he denied Jesus three times (Mk 14:72). Mary Magdalene wept at the empty tomb of Jesus (Jn 20:11). The Ephesian elders wept as they bade Paul farewell (Acts 20:37), and John the apostle wept bitterly when no one was found worthy to open the scroll (Rev 5:4). While nobody is perfect (except Jesus), including all of these biblical weepers, they were all generally perceived positively, and the activities associated with their weeping—prayer, reconciliation, repentance, and death of a loved one—were also appropriate, even holy. Once again, Scripture views expressions of emotions such as weeping, sorrow, and grief as good, healthy, even godly.

"HE HAD NO TEARS"—REALLY?

As we sing in church, we teach theology, so it is instructive to reflect on what our songs are saying about God and his emotions. I grew up singing the hymn "I Stand Amazed in the Presence" (a.k.a., "My Savior's Love" or "How Marvelous!") by Charles Gabriel. Here is the five-stanza version:

(1) I stand amazed in the presence of Jesus the Nazarene,
    And wonder how He could love me, a sinner condemned, unclean.

(Refrain) How marvelous! How wonderful! And my song shall ever be:
    How marvelous! How wonderful! Is my savior's love for me!

(2) For me it was in the garden He pray'd: "Not My will, but Thine,"
    He had no tears for His own griefs, But sweat-drops of blood for mine.

(3) In pity angels beheld Him, and came from the world of light
    To comfort Him in the sorrows He bore for my soul that night.

(4) He took my sins and my sorrows, He made them His very own;

He bore the burden to Calv'ry, and suffered, and died alone.

(5) When with the ransomed in glory His face I at last shall see,

'Twill be my joy through the ages to sing of His love for me.[13]

I want to make three comments about this song. First, it's a great hymn and I love to sing it. But my love for it prompts me to reflect on it and the message it communicates about Jesus.

Second, the hymn is filled with emotions, which is partly why I appreciate it so much. Verses 1 and 5 as well as the chorus sing of God's marvelous love, a topic we'll examine in chapter eight. Several emotions that the hymn describes could fit under the category of joy (see chapter six): amazement, marvel, and wonder. But most relevant for this chapter, sorrow is emphasized in verses 2, 3, and 4: tears, griefs, and sorrows.

Third, comparable to the little Lord Jesus in "Away in a Manger," once again he has no tears, or at least none for his own griefs. Jesus isn't exactly stoic in the hymn, but there is still a perception that Jesus either had no griefs of his own or that they didn't result in divine weeping—despite what the Gospels record. It's subtle, but, at least in verse 2, one detects a negative perspective on Jesus being emotional about his own sorrows.

According to Gabriel's *Personal Memoirs*, the line from verse 2, "he had no tears for His own griefs, But sweat-drops of blood for mine," was suggested to him by a colleague as a possible inspiration for a hymn.[14] The phrase "sweat-drops of blood" presumably comes from Jesus' prayer on the Mount of Olives (Lk 22:44). Gabriel took his friend's advice, but he built on the idea of Jesus' taking our sorrows and added that he was comforted by angels in verse 3 and then in verse 4 he makes them his very own. Gabriel gradually shifted Jesus from having (apparently) no griefs to having personal sorrows as he bore our sins. Interestingly, verse 3 is often omitted from modern hymnals. I realize that there could be many reasons why a verse is omitted (e.g., brevity), but it is striking that the image of a Jesus who needs pity and comfort from angels for his sorrows is apparently too much divine emotion for many Christians.

"A MAN OF SORROWS"

Isaiah's vision of "a man of sorrows" who is "acquainted with grief" (Is 53:3 ESV) certainly seems an apt description of Jesus. When the Pharisees tested Jesus to see if he would heal the man with the withered hand on the Sabbath, he was angry and "grieved (*syllypeō*) at their hardness of heart" (Mk 3:5 ESV). Jesus healed the man, failing their legalism test, but acing the far more important love test. Jesus displayed anger and grief at the Pharisees, as well as compassion and love for the man whom he healed. But Jesus was also loving the Pharisees whom he was attempting to reach. Jesus pointed out the hypocrisy of the Pharisees since they considered it wrong to heal on the Sabbath, but acceptable to plot an innocent man's death (they immediately left and conspired how to destroy him; Mk 3:4-6). In Mark's Gospel, this incident is the first time the religious leaders plan his death. Thus, Jesus' emotions served as a catalyst to the cross.

We see another possible attempt to deprive Jesus of emotions in his interaction with the rich ruler in Luke's Gospel. A textual variant states that Jesus was very sad when he saw the sadness of the rich man in response to Jesus' call to sell everything and give the money to the poor (Lk 18:24). Many English translations omit the phrase (e.g., NASB, NIV, NRSV), but the ESV 2001 includes it, "Jesus, looking at him with sadness (*perilypos*)." However, the 2016 ESV now reads, "Jesus, seeing that he had become sad"; so the sad character is no longer Jesus, but the rich man. This isn't the place to delve into textual criticism concerning the validity of this possible emotional adjective for Jesus, but biblical scholar David Garland makes two comments which argue for keeping the "sad Jesus" phrase. One, Luke often includes poignant details, and two, Luke often reuses words within the immediate context.[15] To Garland's points, we can add that Jesus frequently expressed emotions, including sorrow, so it is reasonable to conclude that Jesus would be sad since the rich ruler appears to not heed Jesus' wise investment advice for laying up treasure in heaven.

Shortly before his death, when Jesus prayed in the garden of Gethsemane, he displayed intense sorrow.

> He took Peter and the two sons of Zebedee along with him, and he began to be **sorrowful** (*lypeō*) and troubled. Then he said to them, "My soul is overwhelmed with **sorrow** (*perilypos*) to the point of death. Stay here and keep watch with me." (Mt 26:37-38, emphasis added)

Both the narrator (v. 37) and Jesus himself (v. 38) describe Jesus here as sorrowful, and his sorrow was intense, overwhelming him to the point of death.[16] And at this point of great sorrow Jesus clearly wanted his closest disciples, Peter, James, and John, with him. Jesus wasn't ashamed or embarrassed about his sorrow, but he freely spoke about it with the three—he wanted them not only with him, but also to know *how he was feeling*. He didn't attempt to stifle or downplay his feelings, but used hyperbolic language ("to the point of death") typical of someone who is pouring out their sorrow to their friends. Jesus is expressing and processing his emotions by verbalizing his anguish, just as Yahweh did in Genesis 6 and in 1 Samuel 15. In Matthew 26 we see another healthy response to emotions, as Jesus not only desired company, but also spoke freely about his sorrow. Followers of Jesus can learn from Jesus' honest and healthy expressions of feelings. He models for us that as we express our feelings and allow ourselves to feel grief and loss, we will be able to process our experiences and gain better understanding about them and about ourselves.

Jesus' sorrow in the garden shouldn't surprise readers of Matthew's Gospel, since in his Sermon on the Mount, Jesus stated, "Blessed are those who mourn, for they will be comforted" (Mt 5:4). In the Beatitudes, Jesus encourages his followers to mourn, grieve, and weep, and then in Gethsemane he models that behavior himself. The path to comfort is by expressing, not denying, our emotions.

In recent years, heretical movements have arisen in some Christian circles, promoting a manly Jesus to address what is perceived as the "problem" of a feminized church. Disgraced pastor Mark Driscoll was one of the leaders of this movement.[17] Here is what he wrote under the pseudonym William Wallace II to "pussified" men: "Have a good cry. . . . At some point you will all learn that I don't give a crap about how you 'feel.' Why, because I am not talking about your right to your feelings. That is the result of feminism, psychology, and atheism."[18] Driscoll connects expressions of feelings to alternative ideologies, but his view of manhood isn't based on Scripture; it's based on a version of toxic masculinity that the church has suffered under for centuries. In stark contrast to Driscoll's vision of the ideal man, the Jesus of the Gospels not only was sorrowful to the point of death, but he also expressed those honest feelings to three of his closest male friends.

LOUD CRYING HE MAKES

And Jesus wept. Immediately after his triumphal entry and shortly before his death, Jesus wept (*klaiō*) over the fate of the city Jerusalem as he foresaw the coming Roman destruction, which took place roughly forty years later (Lk 19:41). The verb for weeping here (*klaiō*) implies loud weeping, wailing. *Our precious Lord Jesus, loud crying he makes.* But perhaps the most familiar incident of Jesus weeping involved the death of his friend Lazarus, the inspiration for the shortest verse in the Bible.[19]

[Mary] . . . rose quickly and went to him. Now Jesus had not yet come into the village, but was still in the place where Martha had met him. When the Jews who were with her in the house, consoling her, saw Mary rise quickly and go out, they followed her, supposing that she was going to the tomb **to weep** (*klaiō*) there. Now when Mary came to where Jesus was and saw him, she fell at his feet, saying to him, "**Lord**, if you had been here, my brother would not have **died**." When Jesus saw her **weeping** (*klaiō*), and the Jews who had come with her also **weeping** (*klaiō*), he was deeply moved (*embrimaomai*) in his spirit and greatly troubled. And he said, "Where have you laid him?" They said to him, "**Lord**, come and see." Jesus **wept** (*dakryō* only here, but a noun in Heb 5:7). So the Jews said, "See how he **loved** him!" But some of them said, "Could not he who opened the eyes of the blind man also have kept this man from **dying**?" Then Jesus, deeply moved (*embrimaomai*) again, came to the tomb. (Jn 11:29-38 ESV, emphasis added)

We should first note that there are a lot of emotions being expressed here, by Mary, by the Jews who were present, and by Jesus himself. The Greek word used for the weeping of Mary and the Jews (*klaiō*) appears three times (once in v. 31 and twice in v. 33). It is the same verb (*klaiō*) used for Jesus' weeping over Jerusalem (loud weeping, wailing). The Greek verb used for Jesus' weeping (*dakryō*) appears only here in the New Testament. (Hebrews using the related noun appears to describe how Jesus prayed "with loud cries and tears [*dakryon*]" Heb 5:7 ESV). Several commentators translate verse 35 as "Jesus burst into tears" (Bruce, Hendrickson)—endangering its treasured status as the shortest verse in the Bible (now with a whopping nineteen letters!).[20] Jesus' weeping manifested his emotions so dramatically that the other mourners remarked how he loved his friend (v. 36).

The Greek verb that appears in verses 33 and 38, translated by the ESV in both places as "deeply moved," is *embrimaomai*, and it gets translated variously as "groaned" (KJV), "greatly disturbed" (NRSV), "moved with the deepest emotions" (Brown), "became deeply agitated" (Bruce).[21] Some commentators perceive anger behind *embrimaomai*, which is reasonable since it could suggest that in its other contexts (Mt 9:30; Mk 1:43; 14:5). But the word doesn't appear frequently enough in the New Testament (only five times) to arrive at a definitive meaning. Here there is no obvious cause for anger, only sorrow. In its root meaning, *embrimaomai* signifies a snorting of horses, so an emotive inarticulate noise. The Greek verb behind the phrase rendered in the ESV as "greatly troubled" in verse 33 is *tarassō*, translated by Bruce as "shook with emotion."[22]

While we might not be able to clearly identify exactly what Jesus was feeling—intense feelings are rarely able to be distilled into distinct emotions such as "this is anger, that is sorrow"—it is clear that Jesus was expressing a combination of emotions at the death of his friend: frustration, sorrow, and grief. And Jesus' emotions manifested themselves in physical behaviors: groaning, shaking, and weeping. The people who witnessed Jesus in this incident interpret his intense emotions, not as anger, but as love (v. 36).

Several commentators note that Jesus' tears prove his humanity.[23] While weeping is certainly something humans do, according to the prophets it is also something God does (Is 16:9; Jer 9:10; 48:31-32). If Jesus were fully God and fully man, as John claims in the beginning of his Gospel (Jn 1:1, 14), then why not conclude that Jesus' tears in John 11 are a sign of both of his humanity and his divinity? In the Old Testament, God's people often weep and Yahweh is grieved and even weeps. In the New Testament, God's people weep and Jesus was sorrowful, grieved, moved with the deepest emotions, shook with emotions, and burst into tears.

THREE LESSONS FROM A SORROWFUL GOD

As Jesus was led away to be crucified, a group of women were mourning and weeping for him (Lk 23:27). Jesus redirected their tears toward themselves as he predicted tribulations (Lk 23:28-31). Even as he was about to die Jesus was concerned about others, and he told them to weep for themselves and for their families. Jesus was not only deeply emotional, but he also prescribed expressions of emotions for his followers. People who claim to be his followers today should follow his example, both of expressing emotions and helping others express emotions. As we attempt to follow Jesus in this way, we can make three points based on our discussion of the sorrow of God.

First, God's sorrow is emphasized in God's Word. The theme of divine sorrow appears throughout Scripture, seen perhaps most dramatically in Genesis, 1 Samuel, Isaiah, Jeremiah, and the Gospels. Biblically, there is no shame about an emotional God grieving, mourning, and even weeping. Likewise, the people of God should feel no shame about honest expressions of sorrow. Because God experiences sorrow and grief, he gives us permission to feel our feelings, to grieve the reality of our pain, and to lament that the world is not as it should be. As we teach and preach the Bible, we need to not only emphasize that our God is a God of sorrow, but also that God's people are people who experience great sorrow.

Second, God's sorrow is spoken about by God himself. Both Yahweh in the Old Testament, and Jesus in the New Testament speak freely and frequently, honestly and openly, about sorrow. As we saw with Yahweh and his prophets (Samuel and Isaiah), and Jesus and his disciples (Peter, James, and John), God invites people to experience his sad emotions. God models healthy processing of his grief, sadness, and mourning. Likewise, the people of God should speak about our sorrow, knowing that it is not only healthy from a psychological perspective, but also godly from a biblical perspective. Our God walks with us through our sorrow, and this understanding should legitimize chaplaincy, pastoral care, and grief and counseling ministries. As the people of God speak like God does about our griefs and sorrows we will create communities of openness that will draw people looking for safe spaces to be real and authentic about their own pain and suffering.

Third, God's sorrow focuses on sin and suffering. God is heartbroken over sin because it leads to suffering. There is an immediate impact on humans when sins involve violence, injustice, or oppression. But then there is the secondary impact due to consequences of sin involving judgment, as we saw in the story of the flood. God is willing to judge and punish, but it makes him intensely sorrowful. Both the sin itself and the punishment make God sad. As we saw in chapter two, God hates sin, but it also causes him to grieve. Likewise, the people of God should grieve over sin because of the suffering it causes in people that God loves. Likewise, the people of God should feel pain and sorrow about all manifestations of sin and suffering. Often these expressions will need to take place in corporate settings where communities can grieve and lament over tragedies and injustices in our world. But at this point allow me to offer a word of caution. Just as Jesus primarily focused on sin, suffering, and death that he personally encountered, it is usually wise to focus on the suffering that we encounter in our lives, lest we become overwhelmed by the pain, sorrow, and sins of the world. There is too much pain out there. It is not possible for us to take on the sins of the entire world; that's a job exclusively for Jesus. Praise God.

THE DEATH OF A MOTHER

About six weeks after my brother-in-law passed away in 2012, my mother, Jane Lamb, died. She had had Alzheimer's for over a decade, so we knew it was coming, not like the death of Shannon's brother Randall. But within a few days of my mother's passing, my father was hospitalized from a bad fall. He had always been quite active, even energetic for a man in his late seventies, so his hospitalization was totally unexpected. Over the course of the next few weeks, my father recovered, but my own health rapidly began to decline.

I had damaged vocal cords for several months, and the doctors thought reflux was the problem, so they prescribed a concoction of medications to alleviate my symptoms. Unfortunately, the meds made things worse, and I started to have trouble sleeping. Dietary changes and a lack of sleep meant that I started losing weight rapidly. Stress over falling asleep is rarely conducive to a restful night, so things quickly spiraled downward into a hopeless cycle of anxiety and panic attacks.

Sometimes in the middle of the day, I would just sit on the couch and weep, over my lack of health, my grief over the loss of loved ones, and my concern about the health of my father. One time while I was weeping, my teenaged son Nathan noticed me, came over silently, and put his arm around my shoulder and wept with me. Just as my son joined me in my grief, we can be confident that our Savior, a man of sorrows who is acquainted with grief, joins us in our suffering and sorrow, weeping with those who weep.

6

the joy of god

Your sorrow will turn into joy.

JOHN 16:20 ESV

RECENTLY, I SCHEDULED A RADIO INTERVIEW for the Monday right after the Thanksgiving weekend. But I didn't write the appointment down in my calendar. Over the holiday, I forgot about it. Before going to bed on Monday night, I looked down at my phone and noticed I received three missed calls from Minneapolis, where the station was located. Then it hit me. "Oh, no, I missed the radio interview today!" Forgetting appointments like this prompts me to wonder if I am slowly heading toward Alzheimer's like my mom.

I'd been on Bill Arnold's show many times (Faith Radio), but I still felt really bad. The truly sad thing is that I have greatly enjoyed each of the interviews I had done on this program before. Bill has a great sense of humor—he even laughs at my jokes (so perhaps not a great sense). We were supposed to discuss the emotions of God.

First thing Tuesday morning, I emailed Bill, apologizing, and asking for forgiveness. Then there was radio silence. No reply on Tuesday. No reply on Wednesday. I felt bad already, but now it was worse. Finally on Thursday morning, Bill responded. "Don't worry about it. Anyone can forget something. I'm a big fan. Hey, are you free for an hour interview today?" He tacks on a PS, *"Do it today."* His reply instantly took me from sorrow to joy. For an hour that afternoon, we had a delightful time talking about God's emotions.

A TIME TO LAUGH AND DANCE

Now is the time to once again mention the "time for everything" poem of Ecclesiastes 3, since it speaks of the progression from sorrow (weeping and mourning) to joy (laughing and dancing).

A time to weep and a time to laugh,
A time to mourn and a time to dance. (Eccles 3:4)

This pattern is repeated throughout Scripture, most pointedly in Jesus' words to the disciples, "Your sorrow will turn into joy" (Jn 16:20 ESV). We mourned and wept in chapter five, so now we laugh and dance in chapter six as we discuss the joy of God.

Joy can be defined as "a deep feeling or condition of happiness or contentment."[1] Synonyms for joy are pleasure, happiness, and delight. In Robert Plutchik's wheel of emotions, in order of increasing intensity, serenity becomes joy, which then becomes ecstasy. For Plutchik, joy is the opposite of sadness. Just as sorrow is often expressed in weeping, joy is often expressed in singing. Among Paul's list of the fruit of the Spirit, the second one, right after love, is joy (Eph 5:22). Paul states that there is no law against manifestations of joy; in fact, people who have God's Spirit will be joyful. C. S. Lewis emphasizes the importance of joy for Christians provocatively, "Joy is the serious business of heaven."[2] As we'll see, our God is a God of joy, and he invites his people into his joy.

WHAT'S WRONG WITH JOY?

What's not to like about laughing, dancing, and rejoicing? In a world of cynicism and criticism, joyfulness is often associated with innocence, immaturity, and naivety. People characterized by joyfulness are often not respected. In the film *Elf*, Will Ferrell's character, Buddy the Elf, attempts to spread Christmas cheer wherever he goes.[3] (MS Word 2013 gives *joyfulness* as a synonym for *cheer*.) Because of his joyful temperament, Buddy is not taken seriously by the people around him, each of whom are somehow jaded by their experiences: his birth father (James Caan), his coworker (Zooey Deschanel), his half brother (Daniel Tay), and a children's book author (Peter Dinklage. Although, Buddy shouldn't have called him "elf" one more time). Santa's sleigh problems are caused by a lack of cheer and an abundance of cynicism. Yet, by the end of the story, Buddy's cheer saves the day, winning over the cynics. While people might be tempted to accuse Buddy of "toxic positivity"—suppressing healthy feelings of sorrow in order to "always look on the bright side of life"—Buddy's character didn't only express cheer. He was brokenhearted about hurting his father, which prompted him to write a note of apology on an Etch A Sketch. The joy of God isn't characterized by a toxic positivity–like obliviousness to pain and suffering, but arises from a genuine expression of delight that often follows after a deep expression of sorrow.

WORDS FOR SERIOUS BUSINESS

Joy is serious business and Scripture includes a variety of words to describe it. I've included table 6.1 of Hebrew terms (for the Old Testament) and table 6.2 of Greek terms (for the New Testament).

Table 6.1. Joy in the Old Testament

Hebrew	English	Divine joy examples (emphasis added)	Other references
tov	good, joyous, be pleased	And God was **pleased** (*tov*) with what he saw (Gen 1:4; GNB).	Gen 1:10, 12, 18
samakh *simkhah* *sameakh*	rejoice, joy, joyful	With **joy** (*simkhah*) they celebrated the festival . . . for the Lord had made them **joyful** (*samakh*) (Ezra 6:22 NRSV).	Lev 23:40; Deut 12:7; 2 Sam 6:12; Neh 8:12; Ps 4:7

Hebrew	English	Divine joy examples (emphasis added)	Other references
gil gil	rejoice, rejoicing	Then will I go to the altar of God, to God, my **joy** (*simkhah*) and my **delight** (*gil*) (Ps 43:4).	1 Chron 16:31; Ps 2:11; Is 65:18
sus masos	rejoice, joy	But **be glad** (*sus*) and **rejoice** (*gil*) forever in what I will create, for I will create Jerusalem to be a **delight** (*gilah*) and its people a **joy** (*masos*) (Is 65:18).	Deut 28:63; Ps 70:4

There is simply too much joy in the Old Testament to examine all the words, but here are the main ones we see associated with God. Notice from the table that these words of joy often appear together. In the next section, we'll discuss possible meanings of the adjective *tov*. The verb *samakh* (rejoice, be glad) is used as a command from God to his people to rejoice (Lev 23:40; Deut 12:7, 12), and in contexts where God is the source of joy for his people (1 Sam 2:1; 2 Chron 20:27; Ezra 6:22) and for his creation (Ps 96:11; 97:1; Ezek 35:14). The related adjective *sameakh* (glad, joyful) and noun *simkhah* (joy, gladness) describe how God brings joy to his people (2 Sam 6:12; Neh 8:12; Ps 4:7). The verb *gil* (rejoice) and the related noun *gil* (rejoicing), speak not only of humans and creation rejoicing in God (1 Chron 16:31; Ps 2:11), but also about how God created his people to be a joy (Is 65:18) and how God is the joy of his people (Ps 43:4). The verb *sus* (rejoice, exult) and the related noun *masos* appear less frequently but are also used to describe God's delight in his people and the people's delight in their God (Deut 28:63; Ps 70:4; Is 65:18). We examined the verb *bakah* (weep) in the previous chapter on sorrow, but it is used three times in Genesis when Jacob and Joseph weep for joy (Gen 29:11; 33:4; 46:29).

Table 6.2. Joy in the New Testament

Greek	English	Divine joy examples (ESV) (emphasis added)	Other references
chairō	rejoice, be glad	It was fitting to celebrate and **be glad** (*chairō*), for this your brother was dead, and is alive (Lk 15:32).	Mt 5:12; 18:13; Lk 6:23; 15:5
chara	joy	You have been faithful over a little; I will set you over much. Enter into the **joy** (*chara*) of your master (Mt 25:21).	Lk 2:10; Jn 17:13; Phil 4:1
agalliaō	rejoice exceedingly	**Rejoice** (*chairō*) and **be glad** (*agalliaō*), for your reward is great in heaven (Mt 5:12).	Lk 10:21; Rev 19:7
agalliasis	extreme joy	You will have **joy** (*chara*) and **gladness** (*agalliasis*), and many will **rejoice** (*chairō*) at his birth (Lk 1:14).	Acts 2:46; Heb 1:9; Judg 1:24
eudokeō	delight in	You are my beloved son; with you I am well **pleased** (*eudokeō*) (Mk 1:11).	Lk 12:32; Gal 1:15; 2 Pet 1:17

In the New Testament, the Greek verb *chairō* (rejoice) is often used as a command or a greeting, "Rejoice!" (Mt 28:9; Lk 6:23). (Perhaps we should try a similar greeting today? Instead of "Hey, how's it going?" try, "Hey, rejoice!") The related noun *chara* (joy) is used to describe a feeling of deep happiness or blessedness (Lk 2:10; Phil 4:1). The verb *agalliaō* (be glad, rejoice exceedingly) is used to describe extreme expressions of joy (Acts 16:34; Rev 19:7), and similarly the related noun *agalliasis* (gladness, extreme joy) is used when God's people are expressing great joy (Lk 1:14; Acts 2:46; Jude 1:24). The verb *eudokeō* (take pleasure in, delight in) is used to describe God's pleasure both in his Son (Mk 1:11; 2 Pet 1:17) and in his people (Lk 12:32; Gal 1:16). Serious business indeed.

GOD DELIGHTS IN *HATTANNINIM HAGGEDOLIM*

At the beginning of chapter five, I noted that the first obvious display of divine emotion we see in Scripture is God's sorrow recorded in Genesis 6:6-7. But we find hints of divine emotion much earlier, in the beginning. We discover foundational truths about the joy of God in the first chapter of the Bible, focusing specifically on the word *good*. The Hebrew word *tov* appears seven times in Genesis 1 (vv. 4, 10, 12, 18, 21, 25, 31), often translated as "good," which is a good translation, but *tov* has a different range of meaning than our English word "good."

It may not have meant this fifty years ago, but the evaluation *good* in English has come to mean mediocre or barely acceptable. If your English paper was returned with a comment of only "good," you would be disappointed, not pleased. Good is like a grade of C on an assignment. On a typical rating scale of 1–5, 5 is excellent, 4 is very good, 3 is good, 2 is fair, and 1 is poor. Good means not excellent, not very good, not horrible, but okay. Would you buy a product on Amazon if its average review was 3.0 out of 5? I never purchase below 4.3. As God evaluated what he created each day, he didn't think the heaven and earth were mediocre—"I guess my creation is okay. I'll give it a C."

The word *tov* has a highly positive, often emotive meaning— joyous, pleasing, or delightful.[4] This definition has profound implications as we look at Genesis 1. The first thing God does after creating light is to enjoy it, the light was *tov* (Gen 1:4): delightful, pleasurable, and joyous. The earth and sea, the plants and trees were all *tov*— pleasurable. God enjoyed the sun, moon, and stars (Gen 1:18).[5] He delighted in the birds, the fish, and the great creatures of the sea (Gen 1:21). The Good News Bible (Today's English Version) expresses this divine delight over creation better than most other translations: "And God was pleased with what he saw" (Gen 1:4, 10, 12, 18, 21, 25 TEV). Walter Brueggemann captures the essence of God's joy here in his discussion of Genesis 1, "Creation is a source of rejoicing and delight for creator and creation."[6]

The phrase translated as "great sea creatures" (Gen 1:21 ESV, NLT) in Hebrew is *hattanninim haggedolim* (if you say it out loud, it rhymes) and could be translated as "great whales" (KJV) or "great sea monsters" (NASB, NRSV, JPS). But it could also be translated as "great sea dragons." Genesis 1 is probably envisioning whales here, but it's fun to imagine God delighting in something like a kraken or perhaps the Loch Ness Monster. Whatever this monstrous creature was, it gave God great joy.

Just as God's creation gave him joy, it can give humans created in his image joy as well. My family went on a whale-watching tour off Dana Point in Southern California a few years ago. The tour operators told us we would certainly see dolphins, and we would hopefully see whales, but they didn't want to over-promise and under-deliver because nature, and whales in particular, is impossible to control or predict. The boat was full of expectant whale-tourists, eagerly scanning the horizon for any hints of spouts, flukes, or breaching. I decided to try to catch a whale on my iPhone, and just as I was setting up to video, an enormous humpback breached in front of me. I caught him mid-jump with the subsequent huge splash. I'm not a photographer, but I got lucky. Everyone who saw the breach screamed with delight, "Did you see that?" As I was writing this, I went back and rewatched the video on my phone, and it brought a huge smile to my face. God created this "great sea dragon" (and all these *hattanninim haggedolim*), and it gives both me and my Creator great delight to watch it leap for joy.[7]

GOD DELIGHTS IN BIPEDAL HOMINIDS

But that wasn't all that gave God pleasure from his creation. He delighted (*tov*) in land animals, insects, and reptiles (Gen 1:25). But what gave him the most joy was his final creation on the sixth day, the man and the woman. Every other object of God's delight was *tov*. After he made the humans, the first thing he did to them was to bless them (Gen 1:28). But then he declared that his creation was *tov me'od* (Gen 1:31), often translated "very good" (ESV, NIV,

NRSV)—which is a very good translation, but in English the word *very* is very overused, which causes it to lose some of its power. The word *me'od* is a strong word, used to convey abundance, often meaning "exceedingly." Since *tov* can mean joy, and *me'od* here serves as an adverb to connote superlative-ness, we could translate *tov me'od* as "exceeding joy" or "pure bliss." To be clear here, God doesn't explicitly state that only the humans are pure bliss, but the only thing created since his last *tov* evaluation (Gen 1:25) was a certain pair of bipedal hominids, which suggests that Adam and Eve are what prompted the upgraded assessment from merely *tov* (joy) to *tov me'od* (pure bliss).

God enjoyed his creation, but what made him extremely happy was his creation of humans. God delights in people. Why? There are many reasons, but from Genesis 1, we see that they are made in God's image, which could explain his great joy over the humans. God delights in us like a father delights in a daughter, or a mother delights in a son. One of the first things the Bible wants us to know about God is that he is a God of joy. This truth must shape our understanding of this divine emotion.

Anyone who has witnessed the birth of a child should be able to resonate with God's joy over the creation of his image-bearers. It is impossible to put into words the joy that my wife, Shannon, and I felt at the births of our two sons, Nathan and Noah. For her, part of the joy was the end of the pain—but it went way beyond that. We finally got to hold, hug, and kiss these two small lives that we had been hoping and praying for. We delighted in the gifts that God had given us in our sons.

GOD DELIGHTS IN HIS PEOPLE

We see themes from Genesis 1 reappear as we examine divine joy in the rest of the Old Testament. Isaiah 62 speaks dramatically of God's delight in his people as seen in this passage.

You shall no more be termed Forsaken,
> and *your* land shall no more be termed Desolate,

but *you* shall be called My **Delight** Is in Her (*khephtsi-bah*),
> and *your* land Married;

for the LORD **delights** (*khaphets*) in *you*,
> and *your* land shall be married.

For as a young man marries a young woman,
> so shall *your* sons marry *you*,

and as the bridegroom **rejoices** (*masos*) over the bride,
> so shall *your* God **rejoice** (*sus*) over *you*. (Is 62:4-5 ESV,
>   emphasis added)

Let's start our examination by clarifying the audience, the speaker, and the context. The message of this oracle is focused on the audience as second-person forms—"you" and "your" (italicized above) appear ten times in just two verses. We know that the audience is the people of Jerusalem since Jerusalem and Zion (another name for Jerusalem, emphasizing its religious significance) are together mentioned six times in the immediate context (Is 61:3; 62:1, 6, 7, 11).

The speaker in the previous chapter was God's anointed (61:1), a role that Jesus assumes for himself at the beginning of his ministry as he quotes from this text (Lk 4:16-21). Motyer assumes God's anointed is still speaking in Isaiah 62,[8] which is reasonable since both chapters mention rejoicing (61:10; 62:5) and are focused on Jerusalem. It is difficult to precisely date the historical context of this oracle, but whenever it was, God's people and land were feeling desolate and forsaken (62:4), so much so that those descriptors became their names. In ancient Israel, your name signified who you were at your core, so desolateness and forsakenness characterized them. Any of us who have felt abandoned by God due to loss, sickness, financial disaster, or relational estrangement could empathize.

But just as God gives new names to Abraham, Sarah, and Israel (Gen 17:5, 15; 32:28), he now gives Jerusalem new names: "My Delight Is in Her" instead of "Forsaken," and "Married" instead of "Desolate." The prophetic anointed voice explains that now Yahweh delights in them and their desolate land will be married. God's anointed one was rejoicing over God (Is 61:1, 10), and assuming the speaker hasn't changed as we move into Isaiah 62, God's anointed one is now describing how God finds delight in his people.

When my wife, Shannon, and I were married, we each took new names to celebrate. She, more traditionally, took my last name (Lamb) as her new last name, and I, less traditionally, took her previous last name (Trout) as my middle name. We now shared the same middle and last names. While our new fish-mammal names perhaps don't have quite the same depth of meaning, they signify our commitment and joy in each other, just as God's renaming of his people signified his commitment to the relationship ("Married"), and his joy over his beloved ("My Delight Is in Her").

The theme of God's delight in his people is found in a variety of other texts. God rejoices over his people a few chapters later in Isaiah (Is 65:19). God is so delighted with his beloved people that he sings over them (Zeph 3:17). Yahweh takes pleasure in his people and adorns them with salvation (Ps 149:4). The God of the Bible consistently finds joy in his people, a message many of us need to hear. Your God delights in you!

GOD DELIGHTS IN BLESSING HIS PEOPLE

While many texts describe God's delight with his people, others clarify that the reason for his delight is that he enjoys blessing them. King Balak of Moab attempted to hire the mercenary prophet Balaam to curse Israel, but God told Balaam to bless Israel instead (Num 22). After his second blessing, Balaam noticed how much delight (*tov*) it gave God to bless the nation of Israel, so he blessed them a third time (Num 24:1). At the end of Deuteronomy, Moses speaks to the Israelites, reminding them that Yahweh will delight (*sus*) in prospering (*tovah*) them, just as he delighted (*sus*) in prospering (*tov*) their ancestors (Deut 30:9). God spoke through the prophet Jeremiah that, after the Babylonian destruction of Jerusalem, he would restore their fortunes for he rejoices (*sus*) in doing good (*tov*) to them with his whole heart and soul (Jer 32:41). Interestingly, in all three of these texts, forms of the Hebrew word *tov* is used to connote either God's delight (Num 24) or his blessing, the source of his delight (Deut 30; Jer 32). Thus, we see echoes in these texts of the theme we first saw in the creation of Genesis 1—God delights in people, specifically in blessing them.

GOD DELIGHTS IN WISDOM, FAITH, AND JUSTICE

God is also delighted when humans trust him and act according to his values. God was pleased when Solomon asked him for wisdom to rule the nation with justice, not for riches or victories as one might expect from a newly installed ruler (1 Kings 3:10). The book of Proverbs declares that the sacrifices of the wicked are an abomination to Yahweh, but the prayer of the upright is his delight (Prov 15:8). The psalmist praises Yahweh because he doesn't delight in the strength of horses, or the legs of warriors, but he delights in those who fear him and put their hope in his unfailing love (Ps 147:10-11). The book of Micah asks, "Will the LORD be pleased with thousands of rams, with ten thousands of rivers of oil?" (Mic 6:7 NRSV). The implied answer to Micah's rhetorical question is no. What gives God pleasure isn't thousands of sacrifices but the doing of justice, the loving of mercy, and walking humbly with God (Mic 6:8). God commanded sacrifices, but when they come from people who don't practice justice and mercy they give God no joy.

In these passages, we see a contrast from what one might expect God to delight in with what he actually delights in. Huge sacrifices don't spark joy for Yahweh, not even thousands of rivers of them (Niles, Amazons, Mississippis, Yangtzes, Tigrises, Euphrates, and Jordans full of oil—now that's a lot of oil!). What gives God pleasure, delight, and joy are when his people pray, put their trust in him, and act with mercy and justice. It shouldn't be surprising that these behaviors give God pleasure because he delights in his own actions of lovingkindness, justice, and righteousness (Jer 9:24).

HUMANS DELIGHT IN THEIR GOD

Before shifting to Jesus and the New Testament, let's see what brings joy to God's people in the Old Testament. Not surprisingly, the source of their joy is God himself. The book of Samuel begins by telling the story of the eponymous prophet's birth (1 Sam 1–2), focusing not on his father, Elkanah, but his mother, Hannah, who had been barren. Her barrenness was a source of great sorrow for her, and the text describes her three times as weeping over her condition (1 Sam 1:7-8, 10). While visiting the sanctuary at Shiloh, which housed the Ark of the Covenant, with her family, Hannah went to pray for a son. Eli, the priest in charge, rebuked her severely, thinking she was drunk. When she graciously replied that she was not drunk, but praying fervently, he blessed her with a promise that God would grant her request. The prophesy was fulfilled as she gave birth to Samuel, and after he was weaned she brought him back to Shiloh to serve Yahweh under Eli. Her poetic prayer of praise begins by describing how her sorrow was turned into joy, "My heart **rejoices** in the LORD . . . for I **delight** in your deliverance" (1 Sam 2:1, emphasis added).

In the book of Nehemiah, after finishing rebuilding Jerusalem's wall, the priest Ezra reads from the book of the law of Moses which prompted the people to weep. Their leader Nehemiah exhorts them to eat tasty food, to drink sweet wine, to share with the less fortunate, and to "not grieve, for the joy of the LORD is your strength" (Neh 8:10).

While the nation of Israel often struggled with obedience, they didn't this time. As they left the gathering they were eating, drinking, sharing, and rejoicing (Neh 8:12). God does get angry and sad, but what gives strength to his people is the knowledge that God is joyful. We are not like the child who feels constantly compelled to make their unstable parent happy. God's joyfulness is great news for us.

The psalmist also describes how God is a source of great joy. The psalmist is glad and rejoices because in God's presence there is "fullness of joy" and "pleasures forevermore" (Ps 16:9, 11 ESV). Because God has bestowed blessings upon him, the king will be "glad with the joy of [God's] presence" (Ps 21:6). The psalmist calls God "my joy and my delight" (Ps 43:4). Isaiah 35 speaks of a joyful vision of future restoration (referenced in Mt 11:5; Lk 7:22). Instead of lions and ravenous beasts hunting them (Is 35:9), they will be chased down by gladness and joy, with joy crowning their heads, so much so that sorrow and sighing will be forced to flee from them (Is 35:10). While it may not be obvious from Isaiah 35:9-10, the context makes it clear that the source of their joy is none other than God himself (Is 35:2, 4).

JOY AT THE BIRTH AND BAPTISM OF JESUS

Perhaps what prompted Lewis to state that "joy is the serious business of heaven" is how many times the topic appears in the New Testament (the words *joy*, *joyful*, *joyfully*, and *rejoice* appear a total of 109 times in the NIV).[9] From Jesus's birth, throughout his ministry, and until his death and resurrection, Jesus prompted great joy in those who were close to him.[10] When Mary, pregnant with Jesus, arrived to visit her pregnant relative, Elizabeth declared to Mary, "The baby in my womb leaped for **joy** (*agalliasis*)" (Lk 1:44). John, the baptizing baby boy, was delighted to meet his cousin Jesus.[11] In response to Elizabeth's words of blessing just a few verses later, Mary sings a poem of praise which echoes Hannah's song of 1 Samuel 2, "my spirit **rejoices** (*agalliaō*) in God my Savior" (Lk 1:47).[12] The angel who spoke to the shepherds announcing Jesus' birth brought them "good news of great **joy** (*chara*)" (Lk 2:10 ESV). When the wise men saw the star stop, leading them to Jesus' birthplace, "they **rejoiced** (*chairō*) exceedingly with great **joy** (*chara*)" (Mt 2:10 ESV, emphasis added). Great joy surrounded the birth of Jesus (who presumably started crying soon afterward).

When adult Jesus was baptized by adult John in the Jordan, his Father declared from heaven, "You are my dearly loved Son, and you bring me great joy (*eudokeō*)" (Mk 1:11 NLT). God the Father not only loved God the Son, but also greatly delighted in the Son. After a report arrives informing them that Jesus was now also baptizing, John the Baptist's disciples express concern to their master, assuming he would be angry or jealous (Jn 3:26). John replies that he doesn't share their concern, but he is like the friend of the bridegroom who **rejoices** as the bridegroom's voice: "This **joy** (*chara*) of mine is now complete" (Jn 3:27-29 ESV, emphasis added). John's behavior offers a lesson to any of us who struggle with jealousy in ministry. As we increasingly find our joy in what gives God joy, we will celebrate the successes of those whom we may have viewed as rivals in the past. We rejoice whenever God's kingdom advances.

JOY IN THE PARABLES OF JESUS

Jesus' parables ring with joy. Jesus compares people who find the kingdom of heaven to a man who finds a treasure in a field and "in his joy" (*chara*) buys that field (Mt 13:44). The cost is huge—the man sells everything—but it is worth it because the treasure of relationship with Jesus has infinite value, which explains his immense joy in making this expensive transaction. In Jesus' parable of the talents, the two servants who double their master's investment are both invited to "enter into the **joy**" (*chara*) of their master (Mt 25:21, 23, emphasis added). Whether we decide the master of the parable is meant to be Jesus or God the Father, it is clear that faithful servants will share God's joy. Joy shows up four times in four verses in Jesus' two parables of lost things in Luke 15. The shepherd and the coin owner are like God who when he finds a lost sinner invites friends and neighbors to "**rejoice with**" (*synchairō*) him (Lk 15:6, 9, emphasis added). Jesus then explains that even for one repentant sinner there is **joy** (*chara*) in heaven (Lk 15:7, 10). Lest we forget, parables were made-up stories illustrating a point. For Jesus, he wanted his listeners to know that joy was a defining characteristic of God's kingdom. When I was in campus ministry with InterVarsity, whenever a student converted, the fellowship always threw a "joy in heaven" party, an earthly reflection of the heavenly reality. Our God rejoices in finding lost sheep.

JOY IN THE MINISTRY OF JESUS

Jesus' ministry was also characterized by joy. After Jesus healed a women who was crippled, the entire crowd rejoiced (*chairō*; Lk 13:17). When Jesus invited himself over for lunch, Zacchaeus welcomed him joyfully (*chairō*; Lk 19:6). During Jesus' triumphal entry into Jerusalem, the crowd praised God joyfully (*chairō*; Lk 19:37). Wherever he went, Jesus brought joy. He wants to bring joy into our lives today.

Jesus sent out seventy of his followers to heal and preach, and they returned with joy (*chara*) because even the demons submitted to them in Jesus' name (Lk 10:17). Jesus redirects their joy (*chairō*) away from demonic submission toward heavenly admission—that their names are written in heaven (Lk 10:20). Jesus then praised God full of joy (*agalliaō*) in the Holy Spirit (Lk 10:21).

Shortly before his death, Jesus wanted to be sure that his joy would be passed on to his followers. While exhorting his disciples to keep his commandments, Jesus explains that he is telling them this so that his joy (*chara*) would be in them and that their joy (*chara*) would be full (Jn 15:11). Jesus also tells them that they will be sad when he is gone, but that their sorrow will turn into joy (*chara*), repeating the theme of joy (*chara* and *chairō*) five times in five verses (Jn 16:20-22, 24). Weeping comes before laughing, mourning comes before dancing, sorrow comes before joy.

Jesus' predictions of joy are fulfilled post-resurrection. While running back from the empty tomb to inform the disciples, Mary Magdalene and the other Mary (perhaps the mother of James and John) experienced emotions of fear but also great joy (*chara*; Mt 28:7-8). The disciples rejoiced (*chairō*) when Jesus appeared to them and showed him his hands and feet (Jn 20:20). After Jesus ascended to heaven, the disciples returned to Jerusalem with great joy (*chara*; Lk 24:52). The book of Hebrews informs us that it was for the joy (*chara*) set before him that Jesus endured the cross (Heb 12:2).

REJOICING IN FLOGGINGS, STONINGS, AND SHIPWRECKS

What does it mean for followers of Jesus to be people of joy? Paul helps us here. His familiar command, "Rejoice (*chairō*) in the Lord always. I will say it again: Rejoice" (Phil 4:4) was not only relevant for his original audience at Philippi, but also for all of us today in a world of increasing anxiety, stress, and chaos. If anyone had reason not to rejoice, it was Paul. He experienced hunger, thirst, nakedness, beatings, homelessness, persecution, slander (1 Cor 4:11-13), imprisonment, more beatings, floggings, a stoning, and shipwrecks (2 Cor 11:23-27). I struggle to find reasons to rejoice, and my life is so much easier than Paul's was (although I do get hungry occasionally). While one might be tempted to interpret Paul's admonition to rejoice always as toxic positivity, the man also freely wept and told his readers about his tears (2 Cor 2:4; Phil 3:18). He knew that tears often preceded joy (2 Tim 1:4).

Joy was not only what Paul experienced, but also what he commanded for other followers of Jesus. Why joy? Because he knew that he was involved in something truly significant. He was seeking the kingdom of God. Paul knew, perhaps from Jesus' words in the Sermon on the Mount, that he could rejoice in the midst of pain, suffering, and persecution because his reward was great in heaven (Mt 5:11-12). Joy sustained Paul, and he hoped it would sustain others as well.

THE PLAY

Many sports writers have called it the greatest football play of all time.[13] If you google "The Play," it's the first thing that comes up. I was there.

It was John Elway's final college game for Stanford. Elway was the Tom Brady of the 1990s (played in five Super Bowls, won two; okay, so not quite Brady). Elway and I were both econ majors, although he was a year ahead of me at Stanford, and we weren't exactly friends. It was a road game, as the Stanford Cardinal took a short trip across the San Francisco Bay to play our biggest rivals, the University of California Golden Bears, in the eighty-fifth annual "Big Game."

There is a little controversy over the result, but I'll begin with what is indisputable. At halftime Cal was ahead 10-0, but two touchdown passes by Elway gave the Cardinal a 14-10 lead. A field goal and a touchdown (with a missed extra point) put the Bears back on top 19-14. After a Cardinal field goal to close the gap, Cal led 19-17. With less than two minutes left, John Elway overcame a fourth and seventeen on the Stanford 13-yard line and proceeded to lead his team deep into Cal territory. Stanford was able to kick a field goal to take the lead 20-19 with eight seconds remaining. Along with thousands of other Stanford fans, I was elated, celebrating what would soon be a dramatic victory . . . or so I thought.

The Cal radio announcer proclaimed, "Only a miracle could save the Bears." Exactly what happened next is open to interpretation. I'll tell you what I saw. Due to an unsportsmanlike conduct penalty on the previous play, Stanford kicked off at their own twenty-five yard line. It was a squib kick, picked up by Cal's Kevin Moen, who lateraled the ball to Richard Rogers, who lateraled to Dwight Garner, whose knee hit the ground before he lateraled to Mariet Ford, who lateraled the ball forward to Moen, who ran past the Stanford Band who had come onto the field (because the game should have been over), into the end zone before he smashed into band member Gary Tyrrell, crushing his trombone (which now rests in the College Football Hall of Fame). A miracle saved the Bears.[14]

My joy suddenly turned into sorrow. I left that game devastated, depressed.

However, it wasn't just a miracle for the Bears; it was actually a miracle for me. While I would never have said it then, The Play was a gift of God to me spiritually. As I reflected on why my sorrow that day was so intense, God made it clear that sports was a big idol for me. My pursuit of sports took my time, my money, my energy, my passion—it was my primary source of joy. But only God can give us true joy and he spoke to me about reordering my priorities. The fact that my idol had let me down so dramatically made me quite receptive to this message.

After three years of attending every home game, I felt like God was leading me not to get tickets for my senior year. I decided to skip Stanford football games. It felt costly when my friends were going to the game without me. (Without Elway—and me—that year the team was 1-10). But my senior year was my best year of ministry. Season tickets for students weren't that expensive, but I did have a little more money. I had more time because I wasn't spending my entire Saturday at the stadium. I had more energy because I wasn't exhausted from a devastating loss or even an exhilarating win. Over the course of that year, I found so much joy in ministry that I sensed that God was calling me into Christian ministry. God spoke to me through The Play. My sorrow was turned into joy.

For many of us, sports can be a source of great joy or great sorrow. The Bible calls anything that we pursue to find ultimate joy in other than God an idol. And sports is one of the biggest idolatries in American culture and the world. We call our sports heroes (Tom Brady, Lebron James, Lionel Messi) our idols. I continue to watch sports and, when my body allows it, to play sports. But when we look to sports—or anything other than God—as our sustaining source of joy, we will be disappointed in the long run. The thrill of victory will always be followed by the agony of defeat. Seeking God's kingdom first, however, will ultimately turn mourning into dancing, and sorrow into joy.

7

the compassion of god

For the LORD comforts his people and will have
compassion on his afflicted ones.

ISAIAH 49:13

IN THE ALFRED HITCHCOCK FILM *I Confess* (1953), Father
Logan (Montgomery Clift) is a priest who employs a German immigrant couple as his parish caretaker and housekeeper (spoiler alert).[1]
One night, the husband, Keller, asks Father Logan to hear his confession. Keller confesses that, in an attempted theft, he killed a lawyer
named Villette. Both before and after the confession, Keller takes
steps to frame Father Logan for the murder. When the police suspect
Father Logan, the priest can't defend himself since confessional information cannot be disclosed. When questioned by investigators, the
silence of the priest increases the probability of his guilt in their eyes.

At the murder trial, Keller testifies against Father Logan, but the
priest again refuses to implicate Keller. The priest is eventually found
not guilty due to lack of evidence, but the mob outside is convinced
he's guilty and threaten him, prompting Keller's wife to declare the
priest's innocence. Keller, witnessing his wife's declaration, shoots
her and flees. The police and Father Logan follow Keller into a large
hotel nearby, where Keller is trapped in the ballroom. Keller,

believing that Father Logan broke the confessional seal and betrayed him to the police, accuses the priest of hypocrisy and admits his own guilt for the murder. Father Logan approaches Keller to convince him to put away his weapon. Keller shoots at Logan, but is shot by a police sharpshooter. While dying, Keller asks the priest for forgiveness. Father Logan absolves him.

The power of this story centers not only on the priest's integrity for not breaking the confessional seal to protect himself, but also on his costly compassion toward a man who first attempted to ruin his life and then tried to kill him. This film came out only a few years after World War II, when anti-German sentiment was strong, making the priest's compassionate acts toward a poor German immigrant even more dramatic. Compassion feels weak, but it is powerful. I weep every time I watch this film.

COMPASSION DEFINED

Compassion is defined as "a feeling of distress and pity for the suffering or misfortune of others."[2] But genuine compassion is not merely a feeling. True compassion, like all the other emotions discussed in this book, involves action, which is why we speak of "treating someone with compassion" or "performing acts of compassion." Just as sorrow leads to weeping and mourning, and joy leads to laughing and dancing, so compassion leads to giving and serving. As we look at the compassion of God we see that it naturally leads to acts of mercy and kindness for people in need.[3]

A natural question might arise at this point. What's the difference between love and compassion? The two emotions certainly overlap and there will be times when it may be difficult to distinguish between the two. It might seem like I'm just trying to fit in discussions of two positive emotions to compensate for the negative ones discussed earlier (hatred, wrath, jealousy), but there is a difference between these two emotions. Somewhat analogous to hate and anger, love is more permanent, while compassion is prompted by a specific circumstance. Compassion is focused on meeting a need. Love is deeper, more independent of a need, and more likely present in the context of a committed relationship. And as we'll see, the Bible uses distinct words to describe God's compassion and God's love.

WORDS OF COMPASSION

God shows compassion all over the Bible and there are many words used in the Old and New Testaments to describe it, so I've constructed two divine compassion tables (I like tables).[4]

Table 7.1. Compassion in the Old Testament

Hebrew	English	Divine compassion examples (emphasis added)	Other references
raham	have compassion	The LORD is **gracious** (*hannun*) and righteous; our God is full of **compassion** (*raham*) (Ps 116:5).	Ex 33:19; Is 63:7; Is 60:10
rahum	compassionate	For the LORD your God is a **compassionate** (*rahum*) God; He will not fail you (Deut 4:31 NASB).	2 Chron 30:9; Ps 111:4; Joel 2:13
rahamim	compassion	Let us fall into the hands of the LORD, for his **mercy** (*rahamim*) is great (2 Sam 24:14).	Ps 51:1; Is 63:7; Zech 1:16
hanan	be gracious	I will have **mercy** (*hanan*) on whom I will have **mercy** (*hanan*) and I will have **compassion** (*raham*) on whom I will have **compassion** (*raham*) (Ex 33:19).	Gen 33:11; Num 6:25; Is 30:18
naham	move to pity	For the LORD was **moved to pity** (*naham*) by their groaning (Judg 2:18 ESV).	Ps 90:13
hamal	feel pity, compassion	He **had pity** (*hamal*) on his people and on his dwelling place (2 Chron 36:15).	Mal 3:17

The Hebrew verb *raham*, "have compassion," appears eighty times in the Old Testament, primarily of God toward his people (Ex 33:19; Ps 116:5; Is 60:10; Zech 10:6). The related adjective *rahum*, "compassionate," is used exclusively of God (Ex 34:6; Deut 4:31; Ps 111:4). The related noun *rahamim*, "compassion," is again usually used of God (2 Sam 24:14; Ps 51:1; Is 63:7; Zech 1:16). Just as we saw a connection in chapter three between the emotion of anger and a part of the body, the nose, the noun *rehem* signifies a body part, "womb" (Gen 20:18; Jer 20:17), and is linked to the emotion of compassion through the related verb *raham*. The Hebrew verb *hanan*, "show favor," "be gracious," appears ninety times and is used both of humans and God, particularly when redeeming from enemies or sins (Gen 33:11; Ex 33:19; Num 6:25). In Yahweh's covenantal description of his name, forms of both *raham* and *hanan* appear: "The Lord, the Lord, the compassionate (*rahum*) and gracious (*hannun*) God, slow to anger, abounding in steadfast love" (Ex 34:6). This formulaic description of God is repeated throughout the Old Testament (Num 14:18; Neh 9:17; Ps 86:15; 103:8; 145:8; Joel 2:13; Jon 4:2; Nahum 1:3). The verb *naham* was discussed in the context of sorrow in chapter six because it can mean "be sorry" (Gen 6:6-7), but it is also relevant here since it can mean "move to pity" (Judg 2:18; Ps 90:13). The related noun *nihum* can be translated as "comfort" (Is 57:18; Zech 1:13) or "compassion" (Hos 11:8). The verb *hamal* is often used of humans who "spare" someone in need (Pharaoh's daughter in Ex 2:6). But it is used of God (2 Chron 36:15), as is the related noun *hemlah*, for example when the angels forced Lot's family to leave Sodom, "For the compassion (*hemlah*) of the Lord was upon him" (Gen 19:16 NASB). Compassion is a fundamental aspect of God's character.[5]

Table 7.2. Compassion in the New Testament

Greek	English	Divine compassion examples (emphasis added)	Other references
splanchnizomai	have compassion	When he saw the crowds, he **had compassion** (*splanchnizomai*) on them (Mt 9:36).	Mk 1:41; Lk 7:13

Greek	English	Divine compassion examples (emphasis added)	Other references
eleeō	have mercy	Therefore, since it is by God's **mercy** (*eleeō*) we have this ministry, we do not lose heart (2 Cor 4:1 NRSV).	Mk 5:19; Phil 2:27
oiktirō	have compassion	I will have **mercy** (*eleeō*) on whom I have **mercy** (*eleeō*) and I will have **compassion** (*oiktirō*) on whom I have **compassion** (*oiktirō*) (Rom 9:15).	

Shifting to the New Testament, the Greek word *splanchnizomai* literally means to be moved in one's bowels in the sense of moved deeply with compassion. Deep emotions like compassion and mercy were felt in one's inner parts. Jesus is often described as compassionate (he had a lot of bowel movements) using *splanchnizomai* (Mt 9:36; 14:14; 15:32; 20:34). The related noun *splanchnon*, "compassion," "affection" (literally, "bowels"—another body part connected with an emotion), is used similarly in contexts describing the mercy of God (Lk 1:78; Phil 1:8; Col 3:12). The related adjective *polysplanchnos*, "compassionate," "full of pity," appears only once; "The Lord is full of compassion (*polysplanchnos*) and mercy" (Jas 5:11). Two more Greek verbs, *eleeō* (show mercy) and *oiktirō* (show compassion) appear together in Romans 9 as Paul quotes from Exodus 33:19, "For he says to Moses, 'I will have mercy (*eleeō*) on whom I have mercy (*eleeō*), and I will have compassion (*oiktirō*) on whom I have compassion (*oiktirō*)'" (Rom 9:15). The related noun forms of these verbs appear separately describing the compassion and mercy of God (*oiktirmos*: Rom 12:1; 2 Cor 1:3; *eleos*: Mt 9:13; Heb 4:16). The God of both testaments is compassionate.

WHAT'S NOT TO LIKE ABOUT MERCY?

The emotions discussed in the first half of this book (hatred, wrath, jealousy, and perhaps sorrow) are all problematic on some level, but most of us don't have a problem with compassion. What's not to like about mercy? Well, as it turns out, there are times when we might not want God or people to show compassion.

We might not desire compassion when it is shown to our enemies. The drama in the book of Jonah centers on the prophet's desire that the hated Ninevites are not shown mercy, which is why he fled to Tarshish in the first place. And then at the end he waited, hoped, and prayed that God would, despite his compassionate character, still wipe out the Ninevites (Jon 1 and 4). It is easy for us reading the book today to be critical toward Jonah, since—I'm assuming now— no Ninevites have ever done anything bad to us. But we might feel differently if God were showing mercy toward terrorists, sex offenders, or someone who has harmed us emotionally or physically.

I hate it when our dog Arti (short for Artemis) barks at the neighbors. It's like she wants to rip their throats out for doing something as audacious as standing outside in their own yard. Her barking feels so mean, but I think I'm mainly embarrassed that I as her owner haven't figured out a way to control her. I think compassion is not good here, not the solution. I want to punish the dog by yelling at her or putting her in isolation for five minutes in the basement so she gets the message I don't approve. My wife however, who knows more about dogs and more about compassion, wants to show mercy and to give treats as an incentive to reward a quiet puppy. I'll let you decide whom you think is the better dog whisperer.

Another time compassion could seem wrong is when people who are in a comparable situation to us receive it, but we don't. Jesus tells a parable about a vineyard owner who hires laborers at different times of the day, but pays them all a denarius, the normal wage for one day's work (Mt 20:1-16). The owner intentionally highlights the tension by paying the later workers first and earlier workers last. The early workers complain about the equal pay despite their much longer shift. The owner replies to their complaint that he gave them what they had agreed to (one denarius) and then concludes with a question, "Are you envious because I am generous?" (Mt 20:15). It helps me to realize that owner apparently wanted to make sure everyone had enough to eat that day, but I am still troubled by this parable. It seems unfair. Yeah, that's kind of the point of mercy. It's not fair when people get better than what they deserve. But in God's vineyard, we are all like the late day workers. God gives us better than we deserve because he's compassionate.

In September 2018, off-duty police officer Amber Guyger (who is White) shot and killed Botham Jean (who is Black) in his own apartment because she mistook his apartment for hers (he lived one floor above her).[6] After the announcement of the conviction and sentencing of Guyger (ten years), Brandt Jean hugged and offered forgiveness to the woman who took his brother's life. While many people understandably protested that Brandt's actions minimized the crime, I think his act of compassion was a powerful reflection of the gospel.

IT WAS PITY THAT STAYED HIS HAND

In the film *The Lord of the Rings: The Fellowship of the Ring* the main character, Frodo, is given a magical ring from his uncle Bilbo that Bilbo had found when Gollum, a wretched creature, lost it in a cave. Gollum wanted to kill Bilbo to get the ring back. Bilbo had an opportunity to kill the defenseless Gollum with his sword, but refrained. Much later, while Frodo and a group of his companions (the fellowship of the ring) are taking the ring to Mordor to destroy it, he has a discussion with the wizard Gandalf about Bilbo's missed opportunity to slay Gollum.[7]

> Frodo: "It's a pity Bilbo didn't kill him when he had the chance."
> Gandalf: "Pity? It was pity that stayed Bilbo's hand. . . . Do not be too eager to deal out death in judgment. . . . My heart tells me that Gollum has some part to play, for good or ill,

before this is over. The pity of Bilbo may rule the fate for many."[8]

Frodo, like Jonah with the Ninevites, didn't want pity to be shown to Gollum. While it appears that God was not successful in changing the mind of the prophet, the wizard seemed to convince the hobbit that pity was a good thing. As it turns out, Gollum does play a key role in the destruction of the ring. Compassion feels weak, but it is powerful. The pity of Bilbo saved Middle-earth.

GOD ISN'T EMBARRASSED
ABOUT HIS COMPASSION

After the sin of the golden calf, Moses makes a series of requests to his God, where God reveals more and more of his nature and character. Moses requests first that God would not destroy his people (Ex 32:1-14; God agrees), second that God would essentially kill Moses (32:32; God disagrees), third that God would come with them to the Promised Land (33:12-17; God agrees), and fourth that he would show Moses his glory (Ex 33:18; God agrees).

> Moses said to the LORD, "You have been telling me, 'Lead these people,' but you have not let me know whom you will send with me. You have said, 'I know you by name and you have found **favor** (*hen*) with me.' If you are **pleased** (*hen*) with me, teach me your ways so I may know you and continue to find **favor** (*hen*) with you. Remember that this nation is your people."
>
> The LORD replied, "My Presence (*paneh*) will go with you, and I will give you rest."
>
> Then Moses said to him, "If your Presence (*paneh*) does not go with us, do not send us up from here. How will anyone know that you are **pleased** (*hen*) with me and with your people unless you go with us? What else will distinguish me and your

people from all the other people on the face (*paneh*) of
the earth?"

And the LORD said to Moses, "I will do the very thing you
have asked, because I am **pleased** (*hen*) with you and I know
you by name."

Then Moses said, "Now show me your glory (*kavod*)."

And the LORD said, "I will cause all my goodness (*tov*) to pass
in front of you, and I will proclaim my name, the LORD, in your
presence. I will have **mercy** (*hanan*) on whom I will have **mercy**
(*hanan*), and I will have **compassion** (*raham*) on whom I will
have **compassion** (*raham*)." (Exodus 33:12-19, emphasis added)

This passage is full of divine compassion, as "have mercy" (*hanan*)
appears twice (v. 19), "favor" (*hen*, adjectival form of *hanan*) appears
five times (vv. 12-13, 16-17), and "have compassion" (*raham*) appears
twice (v. 19). References to divine compassion appear nine times in
eight verses, four from the mouth of Moses, and five from Yahweh.
God isn't embarrassed about his compassion. He wants Moses and
his people to know he is a God of compassion.

We can make three observations about God's compassion here.
First, God's compassion involves his presence. Because Moses really
wants God with them, he makes doubly sure that they weren't going
without God. And God promises to come with them into the
Promised Land. The word *presence* here literally means "face" (*paneh*),
as if God were looking at them while he is with them.

Second, God's compassion is associated with his name. Hebrew
names reveal one's character. As we see in Exodus 33:19 (and in 34:6),
compassion and mercy are part of God's name. It is not merely that
God is compassionate, but that it is a fundamental part of his nature.
He is compassion.

Third, God's compassion is connected to his glory (*kavod*) and his
goodness (*tov*). When Moses requested a revelation of divine glory,

Yahweh replied he'd see his goodness, his name, and his compassion. In Exodus, the people of God had many opportunities to experience God's gracious goodness as he delivered them from slavery, brought them through the Red Sea, and made a covenant with them, which they quickly broke with the golden calf. Fortunately for Israel, God is a God of compassion.

THE COMPASSION OF YAHWEH
IN THE OLD TESTAMENT

The compassion of God appears in too many passages in the Old Testament to mention all of them, so we'll just do a quick overview. The story of the Old Testament is basically one of God showing compassion to his rebellious people. Moses speaks of a future time, after Israel has been unfaithful, that they turn back to Yahweh, and he, once again, shows compassion on them (Deut 30:3). Similarly, the overview to Judges describes the cyclical pattern of the book: (1) Israel worshiped other gods, (2) God gave them into the hands of their enemies, (3) they cried out to God for deliverance, and (4) God had compassion on them by sending a deliverer (Judg 2:18). Jumping forward to the time of the monarchy, when offered a choice of possible punishments for taking a census, King David wanted to rely on God's compassion, "For his mercy is great" (2 Sam 24:14). Even though King Jehoahaz of Israel did evil in the eyes of Yahweh, when he prayed he was sent a deliverer by Yahweh (2 Kings 13:4); the textual comment echoes language from Exodus 33:19, "The LORD was gracious (*hanan*) to them and had compassion (*raham*) on them, and he turned toward them, because of his covenant with Abraham, Isaac, and Jacob, and would not destroy them, nor has he cast them from his presence until now" (2 Kings 13:23 ESV). Recalling Elijah's prayers for weather, the book of James states that the prayer of a righteous person "availeth much" (James 5:16 KJV), but in 2 Kings 13 the prayer of an evil ruler still prompted our highly compassionate God to respond in mercy. I find this story quite encouraging, since I'm more likely to identify with unrighteous Jehoahaz than righteous Elijah.[9]

Compassion is a frequent theme of Old Testament prayers. The priest Ezra mentions God's compassion three times in his prayer of confession before the nation (Neh 9:19, 27-28). After his rape of Bathsheba,[10] and his murder of Uriah, King David prays, "Have mercy (*hanan*) on me, O God, according to your unfailing love; according to your great compassion (*rahamim*) blot out my transgressions" (Ps 51:1). The psalmist prays that Yahweh will "have compassion (*naham*) on his servants" (Ps 135:14 NRSV).

The prophetic books also speak frequently of God's compassion toward his people. The book of Isaiah repeatedly emphasizes God's great compassion toward his people (Is 14:1; 51:3; 54:7, 8, 10; 60:10; 63:7), specifically how he longs to show compassion on his people (Is 30:18). In most of these prophetic texts, the recipients of God's mercy are his people generally (Jer 12:15; Ezek 39:25; Hos 2:19; Zech 10:6), but other specific groups are also mentioned including David's descendants (Jer 31:20), orphans (Hos 14:3), and even the Ninevites (Jon 3:10).

GOD'S "DAVE" TATTOO

Before moving to the New Testament, let's look at one particularly interesting example of divine compassion from Isaiah, where Yahweh is proclaiming freedom to his captive people, encouraging them by speaking of a renewed covenant, and reminding them of his compassion.

> This is what the LORD says. . . .
> "[The freed captives] will neither hunger nor thirst,
> nor will the desert heat or the sun beat down on them.
> He who has **compassion** (*raham*) on them will guide them
> and lead them beside springs of water.

I will turn all my mountains into roads,
  and my highways will be raised up.
See, they will come from afar—
  some from the north, some from the west,
  some from the region of Aswan."
Shout for joy, you heavens;
  rejoice, you earth;
  burst into song, you mountains!
For the Lord **comforts** (*naham*) his people
  and will have **compassion** (*raham*) on his afflicted ones.
But Zion said, "The Lord has forsaken me,
  the Lord has forgotten me."
"Can a mother forget the baby at her breast
  and have no **compassion** (*raham*) on the child she has
    borne?
Though she may forget,
  I will not forget you!
See, I have engraved you on the palms of my hands;
your walls are ever before me . . ." declares the Lord.
      (Is 49:8-18, emphasis added)

We can make three points about divine compassion based on this text. First, God's compassion guides his people (v. 10). They are traveling great distances, but God the great guide provides food, shade, and springs of water. In ancient Israel, having a source of water while traveling could make a difference between life and death. God makes mountains into roads (without dynamite) and levels the highways for smooth traveling. In all of these forms of provision, we see God's compassion. As the mountains are getting flattened, they are witnessing such great acts of mercy that they are invited to rejoice along with the earth and heavens. Surely, if God's creation is rejoicing, God's people should rejoice over God's great compassion.

Second, God's compassion comforts his people (v. 13). God doesn't just provide, but he sees their captivity and affliction and shows them comfort in the midst of their pain. It is difficult to know exactly how and when God's people originally heard these words of comfort, but fortunately they were recorded so that God's people today can continue to hear about God's comfort and compassion toward his people in times of crisis.

Third, God's compassion does not forget his people (v. 15). They are feeling forgotten and forsaken (see also Psalm 22:1; Mk 15:34). God asks if a mother can forget her nursing baby. The implied answer to Yahweh's rhetorical question is, "No, of course not!" I've been told that a mother's body won't let her forget her nursing infant. But even if the unthinkable might happen—a mother forgetting her baby— God can't forget his people because of his great compassion.

To illustrate the permanence of God's memory of his people, Yahweh speaks of how his people are engraved on his hands, like a tattoo. I've never had a tattoo, but to be tattoo-worthy, I'm assuming someone needs to be rather special. God is essentially saying he tattoos the names of his people on his skin. I know what you're thinking. *God has a lot of people, how do they all fit?* Remember that God is big, so there should be plenty of real estate. (And a lot of them are named Dave.[11] I like to envision a big "Dave" tattoo on God's left ankle, visible when he doesn't wear socks, just below his jeans.) To be clear here, I don't think God's "skin" is literally filled with tattoos. The text here is speaking figuratively. But the message this passage is making is still valid about God's incredible compassion. So, whenever you see a tattoo, think about God's hand (or left ankle) and remember that, because of his great compassion, God remembers his people.

HUMAN COMPASSION (OR LACK THEREOF)

The vast majority of places where compassion appears in the Old Testament, God is the one showing it. But there are a few other contexts where human compassion is mentioned. Isaiah 49 compares God's compassion to that of a mother, and Psalm 103 speaks of God having compassion like a father toward a child (Ps 103:13). In Jeremiah, the prophet warns them about foreign rulers who will not show them compassion (Jer 6:23; 21:7; 50:42). But elsewhere in the book, Jeremiah exhorts the people that if they obey God, they don't need to be afraid. God will show them compassion by giving the king of Babylon compassion on them (Jer 42:12). God's value on compassion prompts him to inspire compassion in others.

THE COMPASSION OF JESUS

Jesus, perhaps more than anyone else in Scripture, was a man of compassion, and we see this most clearly in Matthew's Gospel. While Jesus was traveling through cities and villages teaching, preaching, and healing, as he saw the crowds, "he had compassion (*splanchnizomai*) on them, because they were harassed and helpless, like sheep without a shepherd" (Mt 9:36).

Large crowds seem to bring out the compassion in Jesus, as we see a few chapters later in Matthew, "When Jesus landed and saw a large crowd, he had compassion (*splanchnizomai*) on them and healed their sick" (Mt 14:14). His compassion prompted him to feed five thousand people. What's shocking here isn't just the crowd size, but the fact that Jesus had just heard that his cousin John had been beheaded by King Herod (Mt 14:13). He attempted to get away to grieve the loss of his friend who had baptized him (Mt 3:13-17) and had leaped for joy in his mother's womb when they first "met" (Lk 1:41). Even though Jesus was in deep pain, the needs of the people around him prompted deep compassion, so much so that he was moved to care for them and meet their needs.

In the next chapter of Matthew, Jesus decided he needed to spell out what he was doing for his disciples—they, like all of us, were a bit slow sometimes. So, "Jesus called his disciples to him and said,

'I have compassion (*splanchnizomai*) for these people; they have already been with me three days and have nothing to eat. I do not want to send them away hungry, or they may collapse on the way'" (Mt 15:32). Then he fed four thousand people. Not only did Jesus once again have compassion on people who were needy, but he also made sure his disciples knew what was motivating his actions. Jesus wants his followers to be compassionate.

"WHAT DO YOU WANT ME TO DO FOR YOU?"

Jesus' reputation as a man of compassion preceded him wherever he went. People kept approaching him to ask for mercy, like the two blind men of Matthew 20.

> As Jesus and his disciples were leaving Jericho, a large crowd followed him. Two blind men were sitting by the roadside, and when they heard that Jesus was going by, they shouted, "Lord, Son of David, have **mercy** (*eleeō*) on us!"
>
> The crowd rebuked them and told them to be quiet, but they shouted all the louder, "Lord, Son of David, have **mercy** (*eleeō*) on us!"
>
> Jesus stopped and called them. "What do you want me to do for you?" he asked.
>
> "Lord," they answered, "we want our sight."
>
> Jesus had **compassion** (*splanchnizomai*) on them and touched their eyes. Immediately they received their sight and followed him. (Mt 20:29-34, emphasis added)

In response to their pleas for mercy, these blind men are rebuked by the crowd and told to shut up. Jesus has already had compassion on several crowds, but this crowd apparently thought that helping blind beggars was beneath Jesus. They didn't understand that compassion was a fundamental part of the character of God. Fortunately, the two blind guys were not easily deterred, but they persisted in their appeal, "Have mercy!" While it is possible that Jesus heard them originally and chose to ignore them, it seems more likely that, given his character, he finally heard them, which prompted him to stop, not a simple undertaking with a crowd this size. Their generic request for mercy left room for interpretation, so Jesus asks for clarification, "What do you want?" Not surprisingly, they request sight. At this point, Jesus, because of his compassion (*splanchnizomai*), touched their eyes and healed them.

We can draw three points of application from this story. First, compassion often involves a question. Jesus allowed these men the freedom to express their need to him directly. When attempting to meet people's needs we want to make sure we're scratching where they are itching. Sometime today (or better, sometime every day) ask someone Jesus' question, "What do you want me to do for you?"

Second, compassion often involves touch. Jesus often touches people as he heals them (Mt 8:3, 15; 9:20, 29). Jesus' touch here is incredibly intimate—how many people would you allow to touch your eyes? For me, only my wife, and only when she's helping me with eye drops. (I blink as they are about to land.) Touching others can be problematic, inappropriate, or unwanted (particularly during a pandemic), so one always needs to ask and receive permission beforehand. But when praying for someone, a hand placed on a shoulder or back can powerfully communicate compassion to someone in crisis, a tangible expression of the presence of God. (I don't recommend touching their eyes; although, see Mt 7:5.)

Third, compassion often involves persistence. The blind men who asked Jesus for mercy had to overcome various obstacles before their need was met. Personally, I hate asking for help, and when I encounter obstacles, I usually just give up. Growing up, I was always better at math and science than English and writing. I got Cs in English. Over time I learned that my writing improved when people gave me feedback. But there were always obstacles. People were busy and didn't always have time to give me feedback. ("How soon do you need it?" "By tomorrow?" "Sorry.") When feedback came, it was often critical, because with my writing there was always a lot of room for improvement. ("There's some good stuff here, but . . .") But the biggest obstacle was my own pride and unwillingness to admit that I needed help. For many of us, we'd rather be extending mercy than receiving mercy. But since God is compassion and he values compassion in his people, we'll need to persist past the obstacles, like the blind men, to ask for mercy from people and from God.

JESUS HAD MERCY ON BLIND MEN, LEPERS, CHILDREN, WIDOWS, AND FOREIGNERS

In Matthew's Gospel, three other incidents involve individuals or groups who approached Jesus with a similar request as the two blind men of chapter twenty. Earlier in Matthew, two blind men cried out loudly, "Have mercy (*eleeō*) on us, Son of David!" (Mt 9:27 ESV). After a short interaction, Jesus healed them. (We assume they weren't the same pair of blind men from Matthew 20; the idea that Jesus' healings were temporary feels wrong.) A Canaanite woman with a demonized daughter shouted to Jesus, "Have mercy (*eleeō*) on me, O Lord, Son of David" (Mt 15:22 ESV).[12] After Jesus basically said no, she persisted, so he healed her daughter. A man with a demonized son knelt before Jesus and said, "Lord, have mercy (*eleeō*) on my son" (Mt 17:15 ESV). Can you guess what happened? Yeah, Jesus healed him too. We're starting to see a pattern.

In other Gospels, ten lepers made a similar request, "Jesus, Master, have mercy (*eleeō*) on us" (Lk 17:13 ESV) and he healed them. Jesus had compassion (*splanchnizomai*) on the widow of Nain, raising her son from the dead (Lk 7:13), and on a leper in Galilee, cleansing him of his disease (Mk 1:41). Each of these people were somehow marginalized (two blind men, a foreign woman, two demonized children, ten lepers, a widow, and another leper). People who had great needs were drawn to Jesus, and he showed them great compassion. He also told stories of compassion.

THE COMPASSION OF A KING, A FATHER, AND A SAMARITAN

Compassion was such an important value for Jesus that he highlights it in three of his parables (each uses *splanchnizomai* for "compassion"). In the parable of the unforgiving servant, when one of his servants begged for mercy, the king felt compassion on him and forgave his debt (Mt 18:27). In the parable of the prodigal son, when the prodigal returned, the prodigal father had compassion on his son and ran out to welcome him back (Lk 15:20). In the parable of the "Good Samaritan," the Samaritan, when he saw the half-dead (optimists would say "half-alive") man on the side of the road, had compassion and took care of him (Lk 10:33).[13] In these parables, twice the God-character displayed compassion (the king, the father), once the human to be emulated (the Samaritan) displayed compassion. The power of Jesus' stories lies primarily in the outrageous nature of the compassion, which contributes to the impact and influence of these parables—The Good Samaritan and the prodigal son are two of Jesus' most famous and best-loved parables. We love stories of compassion, and the Bible is full of them.

THE COMPASSION OF PAUL, JAMES, AND US

As we move beyond the Gospels we see Paul and James emphasizing the compassion of God. In Romans 9, Paul quotes from Exodus 33, "I will have compassion (*oiktirō*) on whom I have compassion (*oiktirō*)" (Rom 9:15). And Paul tells the Corinthians, "Praise be to the God and Father of our Lord Jesus Christ, the Father of compassion (*oiktirmos*) and the God of all comfort (*paraklēsis*)" (2 Cor 1:3). And James also speaks of the extravagant compassion of God, "The Lord is full of compassion (*polysplanchnos*) and mercy (*oiktirmōn*)" (Jas 5:11). Because God is compassionate, Paul exhorts the churches in both Philippi and Colossae to be "clothed in compassion" (Phil 2:1-2; Col 3:12).

What does it mean for God's people today to be "clothed in compassion"? Well, we first need to accept compassion from God—to wear it, to put it on. We can often think we are like the early workers in the vineyard, or like the older brother in the prodigal son parable. We don't like to think we really need compassion. But the truth is that we all started working at the very end of the day. We all are like the younger brother who rejected his father's love.

We start clothing ourselves in compassion by shouting to Jesus (ignoring the folks who tell us to "shut up!"), "Have mercy, O Lord!" How will Jesus respond? Perhaps with a question, "What do you want me to do for you?" A good answer might be, "Forgive me, and let me follow you for the rest of my life." Then Jesus will respond, "My son/my daughter, your sins are forgiven. Come and follow me."

The fact that we have been shown such outrageous compassion from Jesus makes us people who value it and feel it so generously toward others. We wear it all the time, like our favorite shirt. We not only feel compassion, but we also act with compassion. So we ask questions like Jesus, "What do you want me to do for you?" We touch people like Jesus (after getting permission). We feed people and pray for people. Instead of avoiding people with needs, we move to meet them, even when we have great needs of our own.

Jesus had compassion and fed people when he could have been grieving the loss of John the Baptist (Mt 14:1-21). When Jesus healed the two blind men coming out of Jericho in Matthew 20, he was on his way to Jerusalem. A few verses earlier, he had informed his disciples for the third time that he would suffer and die in Jerusalem. Right before his triumphal entry, Jesus still had time to show compassion to blind beggars. And a few days later, he would perform the greatest act of compassion of all time, by dying on a cross. Jesus was a man of great compassion.

EVANGELISTIC HITCHHIKING

When I was doing campus ministry in Los Angeles, I experienced God's compassionate provision for me in a dramatic way as I did evangelistic hitchhiking with a student. We had been studying Luke 10 where Jesus sends out seventy of his followers in pairs and tells them to take nothing on their journey because he wanted the compassion to go both ways. Their practical needs were met by their hosts while they healed and preached. I was reflecting on how to apply that text, particularly how to put myself in a place to see God provide in order to rely on the compassion of others, and it felt like God said, "Evangelistic hitchhiking." I soon found out how scary it can be to depend on others in this way.

I decided to hitchhike from Los Angeles to Berkeley (about four hundred miles), where we would hold our end-of-the-year evangelism project. When I invited students, surprisingly only one volunteered to join me. Jin was an international student from Korea. I told Jin that he needed to check with his parents first. When he asked, his father responded, "By the time I was your age, I had hitchhiked all over Korea. It's about time you started hitchhiking." (A little unexpected, that.)

Our first ride was a guy who was in the middle of a messy divorce. We had a moving prayer time with him in his pickup truck beneath an underpass on the 10 freeway (LA freeways require definite articles). Because we spent a couple of hours with our first ride, we made slow progress, and to make things worse we said yes to a ride that took us off the main freeway (beggars can't be choosers). We had hoped to arrive in Berkeley within a day, but now it was after dinner and our last ride dropped us off up in the mountains, near a town called Tehachapi, a long way out of our way.

It was getting dark, there were no motels for miles around, and we were at about 4,000 feet elevation. This was before the age of Uber and ubiquitous cell phones. Even though it was May in California, it still gets cold in the mountains, and I was wearing shorts. We did have sleeping bags, but they weren't going to help much. Some sleeping bags have names like "Artic Tundra" or "Siberian Winter" because they keep campers warm in those conditions. My bag was called, "Living Room Couch"; it was rated to seventy degrees Fahrenheit. I was going to freeze.

I'm sure the town of Tehachapi has many wonderful things to offer, but unfortunately for Jin and me the town also has a maximum security prison. Who might want to hitchhike near a prison? Escaping inmates, perhaps? On roads near prisons they post signs saying, "Don't pick up hitchhikers."

We knew things were bad, so we prayed for divine mercy. There wasn't a lot of traffic, but the few cars that came never went below seventy miles per hour. We needed an outrageously compassionate Samaritan. It kept getting darker and colder. It was hopeless. A bit like the two blind men of Matthew 20, we persisted and lifted our hands up and yelled toward heaven, "God have mercy!"

Suddenly, a truck drives by and slams on the brakes. We run up. The driver blurts out, "Hi, my name is Jonny Martin. I saw you guys out here. I felt sorry for you. It's cold. It's dark. You're right next to a prison. No one is going to pick you up here. Get in." He drove us to Bakersfield, where we found a motel. The next day we got rides to Berkeley (where we'd soon meet "the Hate Man"; see chapter two).

Praise God that Jonny Martin had compassion. God often displays his compassion through the compassion of people. Just as Jesus fed the crowds, raised the widow's dead son, and healed the blind men, God had compassion on us. Let's follow his example and be people of compassion.

8

the love of god

God is love.

1 JOHN 4:8

ONE TIME WHEN MY BROTHERS AND I were fighting as kids, our mom came into the room with a voice of authority, "Stop that right now!" We desperately wanted to tell her who was to blame, who started it, and who escalated it, but she wasn't interested. She laid down the law, "From now on, when you fight, you will have to kiss your brother." Unexpected, but a rather effective deterrent—mutually assured destruction. I had to ask myself, "Do I really want to retaliate? Even though he deserves it, is it worth the kiss of death?" There was peace in the Lamb household . . . for a while.

But all good things must come to an end. A few months later, my brothers and I got into another fight. Boys will be boys. Mom came into the room, "Stop that right now!" Instant ceasefire. "Come here into the kitchen." After getting untangled from each other, we marched into the kitchen. "Here's a Bible. Take a piece of paper and a pen, and copy out 1 Corinthians 13, the Love Chapter. While you're writing, think about your actions."

Over the course of the next few years, my brothers and I became quite familiar with the text, "I may be able to speak the languages of human beings and even of angels, but if I have no love, my speech is no more than a noisy gong or a clanging bell . . ." (1 Cor 13:1 TEV[1]). For many people when they hear, "Meanwhile these three remain: faith, hope, and love; and the greatest of these is love" (1 Cor 13:13 TEV) they have warm memories of a wedding homily. I think of a brotherly brawl.

WHAT IS LOVE?

We started this discussion of divine emotions with hatred ("A time to hate"; Eccles 3:8). We conclude with love ("A time to love"; Eccles 3:8). To be honest, I dreaded writing this chapter. Not because I didn't love the topic, but I wondered, *How could I add anything new to the idea that God is love?* A lot has been written about this subject.

My dictionary gives five definitions for the verb *love* and sixteen for the noun, but I'll just include the first one listed for the noun: "An intense emotion of affection, warmth, fondness, and regard towards a person or thing."[2] Though compassion and love are similar (for more on the distinction, see chapter seven), compassion is focused on meeting an immediate need in a specific context, while love is deeper, not necessary prompted by particular concern, but often involving long-term affection over the course of a relationship.

WORDS OF LOVE

John tells us in his first epistle, "God is love" (1 Jn 4:8, 16). But what does that mean?

Despite the popular perception that God in the Old Testament is not as loving as God in the New, we see the love of God throughout Scripture.[3] Depending on your English translation, forms of *love* (e.g., "love," "loves," "loved") appear over seven hundred times in the Bible (NIV, 762; NRSV, 791; ESV, 745; KJV, 546). Most of these loves are connected to God.

Table 8.1. Love in the Old Testament

Hebrew	English	Divine love examples (emphasis added)	Other references
hesed	steadfast love, lovingkindness	In overflowing wrath for a moment I hid my face from you, but with everlasting **love** (*hesed*) I will have compassion (*raham*) on you, says the LORD (Is 54:8 NRSV).	Ex 20:6; 1 Kings 8:23; Ps 23:6
'ahav	love	I have **loved** (*'ahav*) you with an everlasting **love** (*'ahav*); I have drawn you with **loving-kindness** (*hesed*) (Jer 31:3).	Deut 4:37; 2 Sam 12:24
hasaq	love, attached to	Yet the LORD set his heart in **love** (*hasaq*) on your ancestors along and chose you (Deut 10:15 NRSV).	Deut 7:7

Just as English has multiple words that communicate the idea of love, both verbs and nouns, so does the Hebrew Old Testament and the Greek New Testament. The noun *hesed* appears 255 times in the Hebrew Bible, and is translated variously as "steadfast love," "lovingkindness," or "mercy."[4] It appears in most books of the Old Testament, mainly in reference to the love of Yahweh. This is how I describe it elsewhere, "*hesed* is the best kind of love one could imagine. It is the love of a devoted parent to a child from infancy to adulthood and beyond. It is the love of a committed spouse to her or his partner over decades of marriage."[5] God's *hesed* is both abundant (Ex 34:6) and enduring (Ps 136:1, 2, 3, etc.).

The verb *'ahav*, "love," appears 220 times in the Hebrew Bible, usually of humans for other humans (Gen 22:2; 25:28; 37:3). But it is also used for the love of humans for things: food (Gen 27:4), sleep (Prov 20:13), a bribe (Is 1:23), and evil (Mic 3:2). More relevant to this chapter, it can be used of humans for God (Deut 6:5; Josh 22:5), and of God for humans (Deut 4:37; 2 Sam 12:24; Jer 31:3). The verb *hasaq*, "love," "attached to," only appears twelve times in the Hebrew Bible, often with connotations of attachment or connection. It can describe both God's love for his people (Deut 7:7; 10:15) and a human's love for God (Ps 91:14).

THE FOUR LOVES

In his classic book *The Four Loves*, C. S. Lewis speaks of the four types of love, using four Greek words that somehow capture the essence of each type.[6] *Eros* is romantic love. *Storgē* is familial love. *Philia* is friendship or brotherly love. *Agapē* is unconditional divine love. If you've been around churches for a while, you've probably heard a sermon (or ten) on these four loves. While all four of these types of loves are certainly described in Scripture, for purposes of this book, I'll only focus on *philia* and *agapē*, since the other two Greek words don't really appear in the New Testament.[7] And more relevant for our discussion, it is *philia* and *agapē* that are used to describe the love of God.

Table 8.2. Love in the New Testament

Greek	English	Divine love examples (emphasis added)	Other references
phileō (verb)	love	Those whom I **love** (*phileō*) I rebuke and discipline (Rev 3:19).	Jn 5:20; 11:36; 16:27
agapē (noun)	love	As the Father has **loved** (*agapaō*) me, so have I **loved** (*agapaō*) you. Now remain in my **love** (*agapē*) (Jn 5:9).	Rom 5:8; 1 Jn 4:10
agapaō (verb)	love	The Father **loves** (*agapaō*) the Son (Jn 3:35).	Rom 8:37; Heb 12:6

The noun form, *philia*, "affection," "friendship," only appears once ("friendship with the world," Jas 4:4). The verb *phileō* appears twenty-five times in the New Testament, often with surprisingly negative connotations, particularly in the Gospels. Jesus uses *phileō* to describe the hypocrisy of religious leaders who "love" to pray publicly (Mt 6:5) and "love" the places of honor (Mt 23:6; Lk 20:46). And *phileō* is also used to describe the kiss of Judas as he identified and betrayed Jesus (Mt 26:48; Mk 14:44; Lk 22:47), an act most would not consider particularly loving. But *phileō* can also have positive connotations. It is used to describe God's love both for Jesus (Jn 5:20) and for Jesus' disciples (Jn 16:27), and for the disciples' love of Jesus (Jn 16:27).

The love-word that's gotten the most love is definitely *agapē*, a word familiar to many Christians. The noun form, *agapē*, appears 116 times in the New Testament. *Agapē* is the first fruit of the Spirit (Gal 5:22), a goal to strive for (1 Cor 14:1; 1 Tim 1:5), and a motivating force for good (Rom 13:10; 1 Cor 13:4-7). God the Father expresses *agapē* toward God the Son (Jn 15:10; 17:26), as well as toward humans more generally (Rom 5:8; 1 Jn 4:10). Despite what we may have read or heard, *agapē* is not just expressed by God. Humans are to express *agapē* toward other humans (Jn 13:35; Eph 1:15; Col 1:4), as well as toward God (2 Thess 3:5; 1 Jn 2:5).

The verb form, *agapaō*, appears even more than the noun: 143 times in the New Testament (Mk 10:21). That's a whole lot of love. We are supposed to love many people, but the person we are called to love with *agapaō* the most is our neighbor; forms of the command appear eight times (Mt 5:43; 19:19; 22:39; Mk 12:31, 33; Rom 13:9; Gal 5:14; Jas 2:8). The New Testament frequently calls us to love God with *agapaō* (Mt 22:37; Mk 12:30, 33; Lk 10:27; Rom 8:28; 1 Cor 2:9; 8:3). Not surprisingly, the person who displays *agapaō* the most is God, both for humans generally (Rom 8:37; Heb 12:6) and for Jesus specifically (Jn 3:35; 10:17).

LOVE IN PRISON

Now that we've covered love-words, let's look at a few love-texts, starting with Joseph, son of Jacob. After his jealous brothers sold him, Joseph became a slave of Potiphar in Egypt (Gen 37:28). Mrs. Potiphar repeatedly attempted to seduce him. He kept saying no until she changed her tune and accused him of attempting to rape her. In response to his wife's accusation, Potiphar throws Joseph in prison.

And Joseph's master took him and put him into the prison, the place where the king's prisoners were confined, and he was there in prison. But *the* Lord *was with Joseph* and showed him **steadfast love** (*hesed*) and gave him favor (*hen*) in the sight of the keeper of the prison. And the keeper of the prison put *Joseph in charge* of all the prisoners who were in the prison. Whatever was done there, he was the one who did it. The keeper of the prison paid no attention to anything that was in *Joseph's charge*, because *the* Lord *was with him.* And whatever he did, the Lord made it succeed. (Gen 39:20-23 ESV, emphasis added)

When I teach this passage, I ask the students, "Is Joseph's glass half-full or half-empty?" (Technically, the two conditions are identical.) Students typically start with the positives:

- Yahweh was with him (vv. 21, 23).
- Yahweh showed him "steadfast love" (*hesed*; v. 21).
- Joseph was given favor (*hen*; we discussed this verb in chapter seven) in the sight of the keeper (v. 21).
- Joseph was in charge (vv. 22-23).

Joseph's situation sounds pretty good, but we've read the book, and he comes out on top. It's hard for that knowledge not to affect how we read the story.

So, I then say to the class, "Sounds like his glass is half-full, right?" One of the students finally chimes in, "Yeah, but he's still in jail." Someone else says, "For a crime he didn't commit." Another person adds, "In a foreign land, separated from his family." Then I ask, "If you were in a foreign land unjustly imprisoned for rape while being estranged and betrayed by your siblings would you think, 'God is obviously with me'?" Students say, "Probably not." Yeah, I didn't think so.

And yet, God's *hesed*-love was shown to him in prison. So, what does this incident from the life of Joseph teach us about the love of God? We can make three points.

First, God's love appears in unexpected places. This is the only time in Joseph's life that the Bible tells us that God's *hesed*-love was with Joseph. This is also the first place in Scripture where the narrator informs us that God showed *hesed*-love to anyone.[8] When Joseph was at the lowest point of his life, far from family, with no hope of escape, God showed his love to him. When it could seem that God had totally forgotten and forsaken him, God loved him. In your life, how have you seen God's love appear in unexpected places?

Second, God's love doesn't instantly solve our problems. Joseph's situation was experientially awful. He's still in prison and still far from home. Since his brothers sold him into slavery, life has been horrible for Joseph for many years. And it won't improve for Joseph for at least a few more. However, God loved him in the midst of his tragedy without magically making it all go away. When our problems remain it is easy to forget that God is still loving us.

Third, God's love comes with God's presence. It's hard to know exactly what God's presence meant for Joseph. Was Joseph even aware of it? We're not sure, but we know that divine love came with divine presence and divine favor. As a result of Yahweh's *hesed*-love, Joseph was put in charge of everything. When we first met Joseph he was in charge of sheep (Gen 37:2). Next, he was in charge of Potiphar's house (Gen 39:4). In prison, he is put in charge of all the prisoners (Gen 39:21). God loved him by giving him responsibility wherever he was. And soon, he'd be in charge of Egypt, second only to Pharaoh (Gen 41:39-43). Particularly in times of crisis, look for God's presence, perhaps involving new responsibilities.

THE THREE LOVES

Deuteronomy 7 uses three different Hebrew words, each of which get translated into English as "love." In this passage, these three love-words help us develop a fuller picture of the love of God. Moses is speaking here to the people of Israel shortly before they enter the Promised Land.

> It was not because you were more in number than any other people that the LORD set his **love** (*hasaq*; "attached") on you and chose you, for you were the fewest of all peoples, but it is because the LORD **loves** (*'ahav*) you and is keeping the oath that he swore to your fathers, that the LORD has brought you out with a mighty hand and redeemed you from the house of slavery, from the hand of Pharaoh king of Egypt. Know therefore that the LORD your God is God, the faithful God who keeps covenant and **steadfast love** (*hesed*) with those who **love** (*'ahav*) him and keep his commandments, to a thousand generations. (Deut 7:7-9 ESV, emphasis added)

In his description of divine love, Moses looks both back on Israel's history and forward to what God will do for them in the future. We can make three points here about the love of God. (I know I just made three points, but points often come in threes.)

First, God loves (*hasaq*) his people not because they deserve it (v. 7; see also Deut 8:17; 9:4-6). The love (*hasaq*) described in this verse has connotations of attachment. God was bonded to his people in love. But what prompted his affection wasn't due to something special about them. God wasn't thinking, "Wow, Israel is really worthy of my love." They were puny and undeserving, but he still decided to choose them and love them. As we reflect on God's love for us today, it is good to be reminded that we don't deserve it. And it's good to remember, that when we don't feel like we deserve it, God still loves us.

Second, God loves (*'ahav*) his people . . . because he loves his people (7:8). The word for "love" (*'ahav*) here is the main one used for general love, as we saw above, often of humans for other humans. It sounds circular, God loves because he loves, but remember in

Hebrew the two loves are different words. We could paraphrase 7:7-8 as "he attached himself to you . . . because he loves you." Moses goes on to explain how God's love here is connected to his faithfulness to his people which leads to the third point.

Third, God loves (*hesed*) people who love (*'ahav*) him (7:9). The love of God here is *hesed*-love, covenant loyalty, faithfulness. It is long-term love of God for his people. His love endures for thousands of generations, which is almost impossible to imagine. God's love lasts for millennia. And yet there is a tension between God's enduring *hesed*-love with the condition that those loved by God need to *'ahav*-love him back. This text doesn't attempt to resolve this tension for us. But it does make the point that God is giving his people motivation and incentive to love him, because he loves them.

PUPPY LOVE

Psalm 23 is probably the most familiar and best-loved of all the psalms. The psalm describes the various ways God cares for the psalmist, like a shepherd cares for his sheep. Readers of the psalm can reasonably appropriate and apply the words of the psalmist to our contemporary "pastures." God as shepherd forces us to rest, protects us from danger, comforts and feeds us. Verse 4 speaks of how God is with us as we travel through "the valley of the shadow of death," reminiscent of how God's love was present in prison with Joseph.

The end of the psalm includes an interesting description of God's love.

> Surely your goodness (*tov*) and **love** (*hesed*) will follow (*radap*)
> me all the days of my life, and I will dwell in the house of the
> LORD forever. (Psalm 23:6, emphasis added)

The psalmist concludes here by describing all the shepherding care that God exercises on behalf of his sheep as *hesed*-love, which, along with goodness (*tov*), is going to follow the psalmist forever. Thus, the psalm ends with a wonderful image of God's goodness and love following along at our heels, like a German shepherd puppy trotting behind its owner on a walk.

Yeah, there's a little more to what this verse is saying.

The Hebrew verb *radap* is usually translated in verse 6 as "follow" (NIV, ESV, NRSV, KJV). But as we look at how this verb is used elsewhere, we discover it has a much more active sense. It usually appears in military contexts. Pharaoh pursued (*radap*) Israel at the Red Sea (Ex 14:4). Israel pursued (*radap*) the Philistines after David defeated Goliath (1 Sam 17:52). Saul frequently pursued (*radap*) David to kill him (1 Sam 23:25, 28; 24:14; 26:18, 20). "Follow" is too passive for *radap*.[9] God's goodness and his *hesed*-love won't just follow us, they will pursue and chase us, stalk and hunt us.

Why does this pursuit need to be so aggressive? Beyond simply the actual meaning of the Hebrew verb, the reality is that many times, in many ways, we flee from God. A bit like Jonah (Jon 1:3), we run away from his presence by ignoring him or blatantly disobeying his commands. So God's *hesed*-love will hunt us down, perhaps again like a dog, but this time imagine a full-grown German shepherd sprinting across a field barking at us to prevent us from falling over a cliff or to protect us from being eaten by a wolf. (German shepherds can run thirty miles per hour.[10]) According to Psalm 23, God's *hesed*-love should have no problem catching up to us in time to rescue us.

We walk our dog Arti (a rescued chocolate lab mix) on a mile loop twice a day, where she often gets to meet other canine companions. One time, on a dark and stormy night, we were startled by a vicious bark, growl, and lunge. Fortunately, we were protected by a chain-link fence from this Cujo-esque creature who wanted to rip out our throats. Gradually, we discovered this apparently ferocious German shepherd just really wanted to play. Her name was Tori. On our walks, Arti and Tori started to develop a daily ritual. They would run up and down the fence line together, synchronized sprinting. Does it get any better than that? One day, however, Tori had a canine visitor, Ally, who didn't realize Arti was Tori's BFF (or perhaps she did?). Ally barked, growled, and lunged at Arti (canine jealousy?). Tori finally had enough of this, so Tori barked, growled, and lunged at Ally to protect her friend from this interloper. When we realized what was going on it was actually quite touching. Tori loves Arti. Sometimes shepherds have to bark to protect the ones they love.

LOVE HURTS

In each chapter, we have looked at ways emotions can be problematic. But can love ever be a problem? Well, yes, when it comes in a form we don't wish for or expect. Love hurts when it involves truth, confrontation, or rebuke. Proverbs addresses this problem when it counsels people to not despise the discipline of God: "My son, do not despise the LORD 's **discipline**, and do not resent his **rebuke**, for the LORD **disciplines** those he **loves** (*'ahav*), as a father the son he **delights** in" (Prov 3:11-12, emphasis added).

We may not like to be disciplined by God, but, according to Proverbs, it is a sign of God's love. While it might not feel loving in the midst of it, for either the parent or the child, according to Proverbs discipline is a sign of genuine love from a parent who "delights in" a child. The author of these verses is "practicing what he's preaching" as these words of discipline are addressed to "my son." The discipline being encouraged is to welcome discipline.

How does God discipline us? It takes wisdom to discern, and one needs to be cautious about making a diagnosis, particularly for others ("God is punishing you for . . ."). The best divine (and parental) discipline may merely involve natural consequences. Our health may suffer when we ignore God's commands to rest and trust him. Bitterness stemming from a lack of forgiveness can prevent us from sleeping well. A lack of generosity can contribute to anxiety and worry about our possessions. The book of Proverbs recommends we listen to the voice of God in these types of scenarios for how he may be trying to get our attention, disciplining us like a loving parent.

Paul expresses a similar idea in Ephesians, except he is speaking not of receiving rebuke, but of dishing it out. When Paul talks about unity in the body of Christ, he challenges the church at Ephesus to speak "the truth in love," which would lead them to greater maturity (Eph 4:15). Just as God rebukes his people that he loves, so his people are called to rebuke others with the love of God.

REBUKING YOUR NEIGHBOR

It comes from one of the least popular books in the Bible—Leviticus. But this verse is one of the most popular of the Old Testament, quoted eight times in the New Testament, more than any other.[11] It is referenced by Jesus (Mt 5:43; 19:19; 22:39; Mk 12:31; Lk 10:27), by Paul (Rom 13.9; Gal 5:14), and by James (Jas 2:8). Jesus called it one of the two greatest commands (Mk 12:31), and Paul said this command fulfills the whole law (Gal 5:14). We're talking, of course, about the command to "love your neighbor as yourself" (Lev 19:18). Let's look back at the original context. "Do not hate a fellow Israelite in your heart. **Rebuke** your neighbor frankly so you will not share in their guilt. Do not seek revenge or bear a grudge against anyone among your people, but **love** (*'ahav*) your neighbor as yourself. I am the LORD" (Lev 19:17-18, emphasis added).

As popular as this verse is, rarely is the context of this verse discussed. In the midst of a series of prohibitions against mistreating one's neighbor (don't hate, don't seek revenge, don't bear a grudge) are two positive commands, to love and to rebuke one's neighbor. It may seem strange to speak about loving and rebuking one's neighbor together until we reflect on what these verses are describing.

Who are the people that hurt us the most? The ones closest to us, family and neighbors. When someone hurts us, how might we respond? Typically in one of the three ways these verses describe. We hate them. We take vengeance against them. We bear a grudge. According to Leviticus 19, when we respond in these ways we are sharing "in their guilt"—we're just as bad as them. In contrast to these typical responses, the people of God are called to love. But in these situations, love involves rebuke. The harm that was committed by the neighbor originally in these contexts still needs to be addressed. I like how the New Living Translation renders this exhortation: "Confront people directly." For many of us, this is hard to do.

Lest we think that this type of love is optional for God's people, Leviticus concludes this exhortation with the emphatic, "I am the Lord!" God's own voice gives ultimate authority to this command to rebuke and to love.

LOVE ON FACEBOOK

"Help me, David Lamb," was the message I received on Facebook, from my friend Robert, who was having an argument with a group of other friends on the topic of abortion. We all know Facebook is the ideal setting to have a civilized, enlightened discussion about controversial political topics, where everyone feels respected, and usually one side convinces the other side, so they reply along the lines of, "You are right. I am wrong."

Yeah, that's not actually what typically happens. People are often far more interested in expressing opinions than listening. And to be honest, I've also been guilty on many occasions on Facebook of ignoring the wisdom of James 1:19 (Be quick to listen, slow to speak). And the Facebook interaction that Robert invited me to join was typical, not like the mythical scenario I just described.

While I generally agreed with Robert's position, I could see why he was having a hard time. By the time he asked for my help, it was already ugly. There was a lot of "truth," but no love.

I thought, "What a mess! Why bother? Nothing good will come of this." But I can be foolish sometimes, and it was late at night, and Robert did ask for my help. After a short prayer ("God help me speak the truth in love"), I took a deep breath and dove in.

My first post addressed Robert: "Robert, thanks for inviting me to join your conversation. While I'm sympathetic to your position here, I don't support the way you are going about it. You are making personal attacks on these people you disagree with. You're claiming to be pro-life, but you are not treating people with the respect and honor they deserve as humans created in the image of God. For me being pro-life includes being generally opposed to abortion, but it goes way beyond that single issue." I went on to mention gun control, health care, and creation care as a part of a value on human life based on what I see in Scripture—all humans are created in the image of God.

Robert, to his credit, responded to me and the rest of the group very graciously. Several other friends thanked me for my contribution. Tom, who was one of Robert's main opponents and had expressed some rather radical viewpoints in his posts, replied, "Thanks, Dave. I haven't found many Christians who say the types of things you're saying. Next time you're in Northern California, look me up, and we'll have a beer and talk about these issues." I told Tom I'd enjoy that. But I expect that if Tom and I were to have a beer, I might need to do a little rebuke-love with him too. For more examples of rebuke-love, let's turn to Jesus.

MEAN JESUS

While Jesus has a reputation for being a nice guy, he could also be mean—mean in a loving way, as defined by Leviticus 19 and Proverbs 3. Jesus did a lot of rebuking. He rebuked non-humans: unclean spirits (Mk 1:25; 3:12; 9:25), the wind (Mk 4:39), and a fever (Lk 4:39). The humans he rebuked most often were the disciples

(Mk 8:15, 30, 33; 9:35; 10:14, 42-45; 14:6-9, 30, 37, 41), and the religious leaders (Mk 2:25; 3:23-30; 7:6-13; 11:17; 12:10-12, 24-27, 35-38). Jesus was particularly adamant about rebuking religious leaders about their lack of love. "Woe to you Pharisees, because you give God a tenth of your mint, rue and all other kinds of garden herbs, but you neglect justice and the **love** (*agapē*) of God" (Lk 11:42, emphasis added) and "I know that you do not have the **love** (*agapē*) of God in your hearts" (Jn 5:42, emphasis added).

The love of God compelled Jesus to confront a lack of love, particularly in people who had spiritual authority. They knew the Scriptures, but missed the main point about love.

THROUGH THE EYES OF LOVE

We learn more about the rebuke-love of God from Jesus' interaction with the "rich, young ruler." The familiar title for this man actually brings together details from parallel narratives in three Gospels. He's a rich man in Matthew, Mark, and Luke, but a "ruler" only in Luke (18:18), and "young" only in Matthew (19:22). Since we're just looking at Mark's version, I'll just call him the rich man. Right before this interaction, Jesus had to rebuke the disciples for not welcoming little children, whom he then proceeded to bless (Mk 10:13-16).

> And as he was setting out on his journey, a man ran up and knelt before him and asked him, "Good Teacher, what must I do to inherit eternal life?" And Jesus said to him, "Why do you call me good? No one is good except God alone. You know the commandments: 'Do not murder, Do not commit adultery, Do not steal, Do not bear false witness, Do not defraud, Honor your father and mother.'" And he said to him, "Teacher, all these I have kept from my youth." And Jesus, looking at him, **loved** (*agapaō*) him, and said to him, "You lack one thing: *go, sell* all that you have and *give* to the poor, and you will have treasure in heaven; and *come, follow* me." Disheartened by the

saying, he went away sorrowful, for he had great possessions. And Jesus looked around and said to his disciples, "How difficult it will be for those who have wealth to enter the kingdom of God!" (Mk 10:17-23 ESV, emphasis added)

This story is rich with pathos. The rich man arrives with a question for Jesus about obtaining eternal life. In his reply, Jesus curiously references only six of the Ten Commandments, the "horizontal" ones about loving our neighbor.[12] The man claims to have been faithful to these commands, and Jesus doesn't correct him about his testimony. Jesus focuses on the one thing he lacks. Just as Jesus used the language of his audience when he called fishermen to become "fishers of men" (Mk 1:17), here he calls a rich man to obtain "treasure in heaven." Any of us who preach or teach could learn from Jesus' example here.

Jesus appeals to the rich man's self-interest. He values treasure; Jesus offers treasure. He wants an eternal inheritance; Jesus tells him how to store up treasure in heaven. Jesus' financial advice is quite sound—long-term security, great yields, and no risk. But the man apparently didn't follow it. He walked away in sorrow, valuing his earthly treasures more than the heavenly ones Jesus offered.

Once when I was speaking to a group of students on the story of the rich man I said, "The idol of money and materialism must have been a bigger problem back in Jesus' day than it is today. Otherwise Jesus wouldn't have needed to tell this man to sell everything. Right?" Initially, the audience was silent, quietly nodding their heads.

I continued, "Yeah, we clearly don't care about money today as much as they did back then." A few students stopped nodding and began shaking their heads in disagreement.

I kept it up, "Jesus would never say something like this today, because we don't worship money like they did in Jesus' day any more. Not like today, first-century Palestine was known for its materialism and consumerism." At this point, a few vocal students said, "That's not right. We value money more." I kept goading the students.

Finally, the whole room was chanting in rebellion, "No, we're more obsessed with money and wealth today!" Yep.

Money and materialism is a much bigger problem today, at least for those of us who are Christians in the West. I think Jesus would tell a lot of people, including me, "Go . . . sell . . . give . . . come . . . follow!"

As we reflect on the five-part command of Jesus here, it is hard not to feel sympathy for the rich man. Jesus' message was quite challenging, telling a rich person to give up all his possessions. But Mark's Gospel adds a poignant touch—Jesus loved (*agapaō*) this man. Love motivated Jesus' brutal, but quite shrewd, financial advice. Telling someone something painful, speaking the truth, is difficult for many of us, particularly something as challenging as Jesus' words here. Jesus loved this man deeply, because he wanted to bless the man with treasure in heaven, security that would last an eternity. It takes great love to speak great truth.

While many of us may be uncomfortable with Jesus' words here, he is simply telling this man there is a cost for following Jesus (see also Mt 13:44-46; Lk 14:33). Jesus paid the ultimate price for our salvation on the cross. But he also tells everyone who wants to follow him that they need to deny themselves, take up their cross, and follow him (Mk 8:34), which is basically what he told the rich man here. This is a message we need to talk about more in our churches. And if we loved people like Jesus did, we would.

It would not have been loving on Jesus' part to leave out the message for the rich man about selling all and giving all because he was worried about how the rich man might feel about it. Here Jesus loved his neighbor as himself by speaking truth to the man.

LOVE IS A BAD ACCOUNTANT

Paul also talks about giving all one's possessions to the poor in the context of love, but he makes a different point than Jesus in Mark 10. Let's return to 1 Corinthians 13—the Love Chapter. But I won't make you copy it out . . . unless you've been fighting. The word *agapē* appears nine times in this chapter, everywhere "love" appears in the NIV below. Additionally, pronouns referring to "it" appear another eight times. We will examine the chapter in three sections (1 Cor 13:1-3, 4-7, 8-13; I've formatted 13:1-3 to emphasize the parallel structure).

> If I speak in the tongues of men or of angels, **but do not have love**, *I am only a resounding gong or a clanging cymbal.*
> If I have the gift of prophecy and can fathom all mysteries and all knowledge, and if I have a faith that can move mountains, **but do not have love**, *I am nothing.*
> If I give all I possess to the poor and give over my body to hardship that I may boast, **but do not have love**, *I gain nothing.*
> (1 Cor 13:1-3, emphasis added)

There are four "If I" statements here. Each of these ifs describe something spiritually impressive, a subject Paul knew a lot about (see Acts 9:15-30; 13:1–28:31). Here Paul speaks of exercising gifts of tongues, prophecy, knowledge, and faith, and giving all his possessions to the poor and giving over his body to hardship. Any of these individually would constitute an impressive spiritual resume or CV. And yet Paul says that without love they are nothing, or he is nothing. Without love, nothing else matters.

> **Love** is patient, **love** is kind. **It** does not envy, **it** does not boast, **it** is not proud. **It** does not dishonor others, **it** is not self-seeking, **it** is not easily angered, **it** keeps no record of wrongs. **Love** does not **delight** in evil but **rejoices** with the truth. **It** always protects, always trusts, always hopes, always perseveres.
> (1 Cor 13:4-7, emphasis added)

In these four verses "love" is the subject of fifteen verbs. Love has shifted from a characteristic we have or lack in the previous section to something that is personified, basically, a person here. Love is a grandmother (patient and kind). Love is a humble coworker (not envious, boastful, or proud). Love is a bad accountant (keeping no record of wrongs).

While love itself is an emotion, in its personified form, it expresses some emotions, but not others. It is not envious. It is not easily angered, which suggests, however, that eventually love does get angry (see chap. 3). And love rejoices (see chap. 6) not in evil but in truth. Love is like a great friend that protects us, trusts us, hopes for us, and perseveres with us. If you haven't done it already, send love a friend request.

> **Love** never fails. But where there are prophecies, *they will cease*; where there are tongues, *they will be stilled*; where there is knowledge, *it will pass away*. For we know in part and we prophecy in part, but when completeness comes, what is in part *disappears*. When I was a child, I talked like a child, I thought like a child, I reasoned like a child. When I became a man, I put the ways of childhood behind me. For now we see only a reflection as in a mirror; then we shall see face to face. Now I know in part; then I shall know fully, even as I am fully known.
>
> And now these three remain: faith, hope and **love**. But the greatest of these is **love**. (1 Cor 13:8-13, emphasis added)

In this chapter, love shifts from a characteristic to a person, and now it's a transcendent ideal. Paul describes how each of the gifts mentioned earlier (prophesy, tongues, knowledge) are transitory, temporary. Then he appears to drift from directly speaking of love; he doesn't mention it explicitly for four verses (13:9-12). The implication, however, is that love, which never fails, will lead us to greater maturity, where we will more fully love. He concludes with the triumvirate of enduring virtues: faith, hope, and love. But due to its transcendence, its permanence, its preeminence, love is the greatest. This shouldn't surprise us, for God is never called faith or hope, only love.

A BOOK ON LOVE

In the introduction, I stated if there was "one emotion to rule them all" it would be love. You may have noticed along the way that each of the emotions we've looked at are somehow expressions of the love of God. God hates evil, and is angry about oppression because they harm people he loves. God's jealousy proves his love because, as Augustine says, "He who is not jealous, does not love." Jesus's sorrow and his tears display his love not just for Lazarus (Jn 11:35-36), but also for all of his people. God is so delighted with his beloved people that he sings over them (Zeph 3:17). God's compassion, slowness to anger, and *hesed*-love all come together in his self-revelation of his divine character in Exodus 34:6, which is repeated throughout the Old Testament (Num 14:18; Neh 9:17; Ps 86:15; 103:8; 145:8; Joel 2:13; Jon 4:2; Nahum 1:3). This book on the emotions of God is simply a book on the love of God. While God expresses each of these emotions in different times and in different ways, the only emotion that completely characterizes him is love. Uniquely, God is love.

THE LOVE OF A FATHER

At the beginning of this chapter, I described *hesed*-love as the love of a devoted parent to a child and as the love of a committed spouse to a partner over decades of marriage. The person who has taught me the most about this type of *hesed*-love is my father. Here is how my dad displayed *hesed*-love for our family.

My parents' courtship was not a typical romance. Dad was twenty-five, Mom was thirty-three, eight years older. She was a divorced, single-mother with an eleven-year-old daughter (Cheryl). Despite these potential obstacles, Dad fell in love with Mom while they were both involved in ministry to middle schoolers at their Baptist church. Shortly after they married, Dad wanted Cheryl to know she was loved by him, so he adopted her and became her full father.

Over the course of the next three years they had two boys (Rich and me), while Dad finished up his PhD in physics and sang in the choir at church (he sang "How Great Thou Art" at our wedding). Dad went by Dick, and Mom by Jane (like the old children's books), so whenever friends of mine found out about my parents' names, they would ask me, "I assume Rich is Spot, so I guess that makes you . . . Puff?"

When Rich and I were in grade school, Mom and Dad were in a Bible study discussing James 1:27, which says taking care of widows and orphans in their distress is pure and undefiled religion. In response to the Word of God, they decided to adopt my younger brother Wayne, who was seven (I was eight). Wayne is Native American, from the Lakota Sioux nation. Adding a new member to our family was a difficult transition for all of us, but my brothers and I don't fight much anymore—1 Corinthians 13 worked.

When I was in grade school, Dad switched fields of research, from high-energy physics (think quarks) to gamma ray astrophysics (think quasars). When I told people what my dad did, I liked to say, "It's not rocket science. It's more complicated than that." At the time of my dad's research transition I didn't understand why he did it, but I knew it was a big deal, highly risky professionally. For biblical scholars, it would be like switching from the Old Testament to the New Testament (almost unthinkable). Mom later explained it to me. Dad's high-energy research required him to make a lot of trips back to Argonne National Lab (outside Chicago), which meant he was traveling a lot, far more than he wanted to. Doing astrophysics gave him more time at home, more time with his family. It was costly, but he did it because of his love for us.

Dad was always generous (particularly with his children), and shortly after retiring he felt like God was calling him to give away an enormous amount of money to various local Christian ministries. At a time when most people were worried about laying up treasures on earth, he was laying up treasure in heaven. Dad held various leadership positions in the church, but what he loved doing was co-leading Bible study groups with Mom and teaching Sunday school.

A natural consequence of marrying someone eight years older meant that when he was in his midseventies, Mom was in her early eighties. And like her mother before her, Mom struggled with Alzheimer's for the last decade of her life. During this battle, Dad took care of Mom for years in their home until it became dangerous for her. When she needed to move to a care facility, Dad would visit her three times a day. Whenever my family visited Dad, he'd say, "Let's go see Jane." Toward the end of her life, he would feed her, tease her, sing to her, or somehow make her smile. Dad *hesed*-loved Mom over five decades.

While he was in college at MIT, Dad learned the St. Olaf College fight song from his roommate who was from Northfield, Minnesota. Dad taught it to Mom. Because of the development of her Alzheimer's, their fiftieth anniversary celebration was a little sad, given that Mom wasn't really there. She could no longer converse, interact, or engage with anyone, but she could sing. At the end of the party, Dad stood with Mom at the microphone, and started to sing, "*We come from St. Olaf . . .*".

Mom stared into Dad's eyes and sang harmony to his melody. There wasn't a dry eye in the room. Mom passed away three years later.

Dad loved Mom. He loved his children. But most significantly, he loved Jesus. And as he lived out his love, I got a glimpse of the *hesed*-love God has for his children—and his bride, the church. When Dad passed away in February 2018 at the age of eighty-four, we wept.[13] But we know he went to a better place, to be with God, who is love.

the emotions of
the people of god

For I find my delight in your commandments, which I love.

PSALM 119:47 ESV

THERE IS A COMMON PERCEPTION in many contexts that expressions of emotions disqualify people for leadership. In the Netflix drama *The Crown*, Queen Elizabeth is on the throne. It is the age of women (sort of), as the UK also has its first woman prime minister, Margaret Thatcher. During their initial meeting, Elizabeth (Olivia Colman) invites Thatcher (Gillian Anderson) to set up her government, which involves selecting a cabinet. The queen asks the prime minister if she can first make a prediction.

> Elizabeth: "I'm assuming no women."
> Thatcher: "Women?"
> Elizabeth: "In cabinet."
> Thatcher: "No, certainly not. Not just because there aren't any suitable candidates.[1] But I have found women in general not to be suited to high office" (*prompting a raised eyebrow from the queen*).

Elizabeth: "Oh, why is that?"

Thatcher: "They become too emotional."

Elizabeth: "I doubt you'll have that trouble with me."[2]

There is too much to say about this ironic interaction (Anderson and Colman both won Emmys in 2021 for these portrayals), so I will just focus on emotions and leadership. Some may think that Thatcher's leadership strategy worked in 1970s England—stiff upper lip and all. But in the world of the Bible, God and God's leaders are quite emotional. Emotions never hindered them in their leadership, in fact it enhanced their ability to lead. The best leaders don't squelch emotions. They aren't afraid to feel them, talk about them, and publicly express them.

THE PROBLEM OF EMOTIONS

The previous eight chapters have focused primarily on the emotions of God. As we conclude, I will focus on the emotions of the people of God, specifically how we can appropriately image God as we express our divine feelings. But as we've seen, emotions can be problematic.

What I said about emotions in chapter one (they can seem irrational, uncontrollable, and confusing) could lead one to believe that I agreed with Thatcher. However, in that chapter, and hopefully throughout this book we've seen how emotions are normal, natural, even divine. It would be irrational in light of how positively emotions are viewed in the Bible—for both God and God's people—to avoid, discount, or downplay healthy displays of emotions.

Emotions can be problematic, but they also can be powerful, which is why God's Word calls God's people to learn to control them. And what better model to help us do this than God himself, who not only tells us but also shows us that he is, among other things, angry and loving. However, he controls his anger by getting there slowly, while also giving free release to his love and abounding in it.

Emotions are often hard to understand, but fortunately they are the focus of so much of God's Word that motivated readers can learn a lot about emotions, both divine and human, by simply opening their Bibles.[3] When the problematic nature of emotions prompts us to avoid or ignore them, we lose far more than we gain.

EMOTIONS ARE STICKY

What do we lose when we ignore divine and human emotions? What do we gain when we acknowledge and emphasize them? Even though they weren't primarily concerned with these questions in their bestselling book *Made to Stick*, authors Chip Heath and Dan Heath help us answer them.[4] Their book targets marketers and teachers, parents and preachers—anyone with an important idea and a desire to make their idea "sticky." Sticky ideas have an enduring impact and motivate people to act. How does one make an important message stick in a world of information overload?

One of the Heath brothers' six sticky principles is that ideas need to be emotional. They show how compassion prompted people to give more money to charities like Save the Children and how anger led youth to not smoke. The brothers Heath argue that if you connect to people emotionally, they are more likely not only to care about your concern but also to act on it. Ideas (and leaders) that are emotional are more sticky, and therefore more impactful, more influential. However, this principal can be abused by leaders and media personalities who play on fear and anger to gain power. Therefore, as parents, teachers, and spiritual leaders, we use emotions not to manipulate, but to help people more effectively learn about and be transformed by God and God's Word. The implications of *Made to Stick* are profound for the church in evangelism, discipleship, and teaching. According to Heath and Heath, the Iron Lady would have been more effective as prime minister if she had more women—and men—on her cabinet who were not afraid of healthy displays of emotions.

EMOTIONAL TEACHING

In his book *Small Teaching*, educator James Lang provides lessons for other teachers from the science of learning.[5] In his section on "Motivating," he focuses, not surprisingly, on emotions. Lang shows how emotions help teachers capture the attention of students and help boost student motivation. He encourages teachers to tell stories, particularly ones that invoke emotions. (Heath and Heath also argue that stories make ideas more sticky using the parable of The Good Samaritan as a powerful example.[6]) Lang states, "Stories have the power to induce laughter, sorrow, puzzlement, and anger. Indeed, I would be hard-pressed to think of a great story that did not produce emotions of some kind."[7] While some are better than others, I always begin my classes with a story (followed by a prayer). Many of the stories I've told in this book, I've honed in the classroom over many retellings.

Lang acknowledges that there are clear downsides to negative emotions (fear, anger), but he shows how powerful they can be to accentuate memory. To illustrate this point, Lang tells a sad tale of their family dog and a skunk; the dog "still approaches the backyard with trepidation."[8] Perhaps other dog owners have their own version of this story? Lang shows how recent research concludes that teachers who use emotions, both positive and negative, will be more effective in the classroom. On this criterion alone, Jesus would have been a highly effective instructor.

LEADING EMOTIONALLY

Leaders often think that they need to be coldly rational, like Margaret Thatcher, to make wise decisions. There are certainly times when out-of-control emotions have led people to make foolish decisions. Many of us have regretted tweeting or making a Facebook post late at night in a fit of anger. Not wise.

But in many situations, emotions are necessary to make tough decisions. When faced with perpetual injustice a rational person might be tempted to give up, but a leader who is motivated by righteous anger can make wise decisions that not only take seriously the nature of the obstacles and the need for persistence, but that also provide a compelling vision of a new, just future. When a hurricane or earthquake strikes, compassion often prompts churches to give sacrificially, even though their financial statements might reasonably lead them to take a less generous path. During the recent Covid-19 pandemic, many leaders felt grief, sorrow, and loneliness. The leaders who decided to share about and process these difficult emotions found receptive audiences. In the process, their communities were able to begin to make sense of the tragedy and to connect to God in the midst of their pain.

TEACHING WHILE CRYING

Pastors and other leaders sometimes use contrived emotions to manipulate others, which should cause us to pause and perhaps ask for feedback about our leadership style. But since Jesus and other biblical leaders led emotionally, we need to learn how to do so as well. Authentic and vulnerable expressions of emotion can help leaders connect powerfully with their audiences to motivate in a healthy, even godly, way. Leaders who express emotions freely and vulnerably model for those around them that emotions are real, normal, and valid. Over time, as pastors and teachers routinely express their feelings in healthy ways, safe spaces will be cultivated in their small groups, Sunday school classes, and congregations for people to share honestly and openly about their struggles, sorrows, and joys. Communities like this are a foretaste of heaven.

One time I was teaching the Old Testament in the midst of a personal health crisis. It wasn't part of my lecture notes, but I spontaneously ended up sharing with my students about my pain, my stress, and my confusion over why God wasn't healing me. I wept.

Immediately afterward, I felt embarrassed about my "inappropriate" display of emotion. I thought, I just won't mention it again and maybe the students will forget. They didn't. At the end of the class, several students told me that my tears were the most powerful lesson they took away from the class. Their comments confirmed what I should have known from Scripture. Biblical leaders are not afraid of emotions, but display them openly and honestly.

THE DUAL-HATTED MESSIAH

Often when people talk about Jesus displaying emotions they say we are seeing his human side. It is almost like Jesus has two hats, the human hat and the divine hat. He puts on his divine hat to heal the sick, calm storms, and read people's minds. Only God could do those things. He puts on his human hat when he weeps, gets angry, or expresses joy—any time he is emotional. The common perception is that God doesn't display emotions, but humans do.

I have a problem with the two-hat theory of Jesus. At the very least this perception is misleading, but depending on how it is expressed, it may be heretical. Jesus always wears both his divine hat and his human hat—he is the Dual-Hatted Messiah. He is always fully divine and fully human.[9] When Jesus gets emotional it's not like he is somehow more human at that point. We could almost say Jesus was more divine when he was expressing emotions (if that weren't also heretical). As we've seen from the actions and descriptions of Yahweh in the Old Testament, and Jesus in the New, the God of the Bible is profoundly, intensely, genuinely emotional. Therefore, as image-bearers of God, and as followers of Jesus, the people of God will also weep, get angry, and express joy.

HATE AND LOVE IN PSALM 119

In the first chapter, we looked at a psalm that mentions all seven emotions focused on in this book, Psalm 69. There is another psalm that mentions all seven, Psalm 119. While the person primarily experiencing the emotions in Psalm 69 is God, in Psalm 119 it is primarily the psalmist. As we conclude by reflecting on what it means to us to appropriately image God's emotions, this beloved (and long!) psalm helps us.

I won't include all 176 verses, but here is a sample of verses (emphasis added) that mention these seven emotions.

- **Hate:** "I **hate** (*sana'*) and abhor falsehood, but I **love** (*'ahav*) your law" (v. 163 ESV). Forms of hate (disgust, contempt) appear in six other verses in this psalm (vv. 22, 51, 104, 113, 128, 158).

- **Wrath:** "**Hot indignation** (*zal'aphah*) seizes me because of the wicked, who forsake your law" (v. 53 ESV). While wrath appears frequently in the Bible, it only appears once in Psalm 119.

- **Jealousy:** "My **zeal** (*qin'ah*) consumes me, because my foes forget your words" (v. 139 ESV). The Hebrew word *qin'ah* can also be translated as "jealousy" (see chap. 4).

- **Sorrow:** "My soul melts away for **sorrow** (*tugah*); strengthen me according to your word!" (v. 28 ESV). The psalmist also sheds "streams of tears" in verse 136.

- **Joy:** "Your testimonies are my heritage forever, for they are the **joy** (*sason*) of my heart" (v. 111 ESV). The joy synonym "delight" appears ten times in the psalm (vv. 14, 16, 24, 35, 47, 70, 77, 92, 143, 174).

- **Compassion:** "Great is your **mercy** (*raham*), O LORD; give me life according to your rules" (v. 156 ESV). "Your mercy" also appears in verse 77. (Both of these verses are describing not the compassion of the psalmist, but of God.)

- **Love:** "For I find my **delight** in your commandments, which I **love**" (*'ahav*, v. 47 ESV). "Love" appears in fourteen other verses: 48, 64, 76, 88, 97, 113, 119, 124, 127, 132, 140, 149, 159, 163.

Among all these emotions, two of them are mentioned once in Psalm 119 (wrath and jealousy), three of them appear several times (hatred, sorrow, and compassion), and two of them appear over ten times (joy and love). In particular, the psalmist loves and delights in God's Word. But these aren't the only human emotions expressed in Psalm 119. Other emotive words appear with great frequency: hope (seven times), affliction (seven times), longing (seven times), and heart (fifteen times).[10] This foundational psalm overflows with emotion.

It may seem obvious, but it's worth stating: Psalm 119 is addressed to God. The second-person possessive pronoun *your* appears 212 times in the ESV translation. The longest chapter in the Bible is a prayer about Scripture. The psalmist prays through all of these emotions, knowing God hears and understands, because God himself shares these emotions. And the focus of this prayer is on the Word of God. A Torah synonym appears in every verse (word, law, precepts, commandments, rules, testimonies, statutes, judgments, promise). Psalm 119 expresses a full array of human emotions, reflecting the fact that we bear the image of a very emotional God. Our prayers, Bible studies, and sermons should be, like this psalm, full of emotion.

FEEL, TALK, ACT

The main takeaway of this book can be distilled into three points.

One, feel emotions like God does. The Bible speaks frequently and boldly about the emotions of God. Emotions are not something to be embarrassed about, but they need to be noticed, observed, and even listened to. Emotions make us aware of basic needs—anxiety points to our need to feel safe. As we feel these emotions powerfully, we can reflect on what they are telling us about ourselves. And as we reflect, we remember we are created in the image of our emotional God. There is no reason for the people of God to hide our tears or stifle our joy. And as we've seen, godly people in the Bible are emotional and we follow an emotional Savior.

Two, talk about emotions like God does. We know God doesn't stifle his emotions because he frequently spoke about them. The biblical narrator often informs us that God is emotional, but in many instances it is God himself who is speaking about the emotions he's feeling. In the Old Testament, Yahweh spoke to his people and his prophets about what he was feeling. And in the New Testament, Jesus did the same with the crowds and his disciples. Because there is no reason to be ashamed, the people of God follow the example of their God and talk about their emotions.

Three, act on emotions like God does. Emotions are meant to be expressed not only in words, but also with the rest of our body. In the language of the Bible, parts of the body are integrally associated with expressions of emotions. The heart is connected with grief and joy, the nose with anger, the womb and bowels with compassion. Emotions are not to be stifled or merely spoken about, they need to be expressed with our whole body. Yell and weep, dance and sing, serve and love.

As we feel, talk about, and act on our emotions like God, let's remember that God is often described as experiencing multiple emotions all within the same passage. As he reveals his name to Moses, Yahweh states that his character includes a complex array of emotions: compassion, love, anger, and jealousy (Ex 34:6-7, 14). Psalm 69 speaks of God's wrath and anger, as well as his love and mercy. When Jesus heals the man with the withered hand, we assume he feels compassion. Mark tells us he felt anger and grief at the hardness of heart of the Pharisees (Mk 3:3-5). And as we just saw, the psalmist experienced most of these emotions in Psalm 119. Every display of God's emotions is somehow connected to his love.

Returning to the film *Inside Out* (spoiler alert), much of the story within Riley's mind involves Joy's character trying to stifle Sadness's character, despite the best efforts of Sadness to express herself. After their adventure together, Joy and Sadness finally create a joint, multicolored memory of when Riley told her parents in tears of how she missed her life in Minnesota and was comforted by her parents. Human emotional experiences are multifaceted, just like God's (and Riley's).

A LOVE FOR GOD'S WORD

It was the first day of class and the professor, J. Robert Clinton, placed a piece of paper on everyone's desk with a simple image of a tombstone. "Your assignment for Thursday is to write your epitaph for your tombstone. What do you want people to say about you when you're dead?"

At that point in my life, I was still in my midthirties. I thought, "Isn't it a little early to start thinking about my death? I think I've got a few more good decades left in me."

The professor was reading my mind, "It's never too early to start thinking about your death. What you want people to say about you after you're gone should impact how you live your life today." So, I guess I should start working on my tombstone.

It was the easiest assignment I'd ever had—only one sentence. It was the hardest assignment I'd ever had—only my entire life. I struggled, prayed, brainstormed with my wife, Shannon, over the next forty-eight hours. Finally, it was like God spoke to me:

He loved to give others a love for God's Word.

Those words fit my life thus far, and I hoped and prayed it would fit my life over the course of the subsequent decades. As I write this, it was twenty-five years ago. I certainly have many flaws as a teacher, but one of my strengths is passion. It's the positive comment that appears most frequently on course evaluations, "Dr. Lamb's passion helped me gain a love for the Old Testament."

I find that passing on my love for Scripture is one of the best ways for me to love others, because as we delve into it, we discover that

God is love. And my hope and prayer for this book is that it will somehow help readers grow in love for God, for God's people, and for God's Word. From the Word of God we learn how to feel, talk about, and express emotions, and thereby we connect to our emotional God.

acknowledgments

GENERALLY, THE MORE PEOPLE INVOLVED in the process of writing a book, the better it is. Many great folks contributed to this one.

I get most of my best ideas in communities of learning, and I've been privileged to teach this material with students at Missio Seminary, with our small group (Leah, Walt, Don, Maggie, Carol, Keith, Mike, and Sue), and with our Sunday school class (The Gathering) at Calvary Church of Souderton. Each of these groups of people offered wisdom and perspective, and helped me better understand emotions, both human and divine.

My editors at InterVarsity Press, Al Hsu and Rachel Hastings, gave me extensive feedback, pushing this Bible nerd to include more stories and practical application, things I wanted to do, but needed help to accomplish. My spiritual director, Christine Labrum, asked me probing questions along the way, allowing me to express and reflect on my own emotions, and connect more deeply with God in the process. Former student and current colleague Jason Armold blessed me with great feedback on several chapters, as he has done with other books. Frank James and Todd Mangum from Missio granted me the privilege to take a Sabbatical in the fall of 2021 which allowed me time to finish the first draft.

The people who have helped me not only edit and revise this book, but express and understand my emotions the most are my family. My wife, Shannon, and my sons, Nathan and Noah, brainstormed stories, songs, and films which will hopefully help readers connect more deeply with the subject matter. I have particularly appreciated utilizing the psychology background of Nathan to help me talk about human emotions with greater sensitivity and insight. I have learned over three decades of marriage that when it comes to editing, I ignore the wisdom of my wise wife at my own peril. She is a gift from God to me.

My parents have not only helped me understand God better, but, with the exception of hatred and jealousy, they have also prompted me to feel the full array of emotions discussed in this book, most significantly, great sorrow and grief at their passing. This book is dedicated to their memory.

Appendix

comparing the emotions of god

THIS TABLE SUMMARIZES AND COMPARES the seven emotions discussed in this book. For four of the emotions (hatred, wrath, sorrow, and joy), I include Robert Plutchik's scale of increasing emotional intensity. The list of Hebrew and Greek words only includes a sample of two-to-four words per emotion (Greek words are underlined).

Table A.1. Comparing the emotions of God

Emotion	Hebrew, <u>Greek</u> words	Definition	Comparison to other emotions	Examples (emphasis added)
Hatred	*sana'* *sin'ah* <u>*miseō*</u>	To feel strong dislike or disgust.	Robert Plutchik: boredom ➡ disgust ➡ loathing. Hatred is deeper than wrath and tends to last longer.	I **hate** (*sana'*), I despise your religious festivals; your assemblies are a stench to me (Amos 5:21 ESV).
Wrath	*'ap* *hemah* <u>*orgē*</u> <u>*thymos*</u>	A strong feeling of annoyance, antagonism, or displeasure resulting from grievance or opposition.	Plutchik: annoyance ➡ anger ➡ rage. Somewhat distinct from hatred, anger is often triggered by a specific act.	He also will drink the wine of God's **wrath** (*thymos*) (Rev 14:10 ESV).

Emotion	Hebrew, <u>Greek</u> words	Definition	Comparison to other emotions	Examples (emphasis added)
Jealousy	*qanna'* <u>*zēlos*</u>	Healthy jealousy is a desire for something that is rightfully yours.	In contrast to jealousy, envy is a desire for something that is not yours to have.	For I the LORD your God am a **jealous** (*qanna'*) God (Ex 20:5 ESV).
Sorrow	*naham* *'atsav* <u>*lypeō*</u> <u>*klaiō*</u>	A feeling caused by a negative circumstance (pain, sin, death).	Plutchik: pensiveness ➡ sadness ➡ grief.	He began to be **sorrowful** (*lypeō*) and troubled (Mt 26:37 ESV).
Joy	*tov* *samakh* <u>*chairō*</u> <u>*eudokeō*</u>	A deep feeling or condition of happiness.	Plutchik: serenity ➡ joy ➡ ecstasy.	And God was **pleased** (*tov*) with what he saw (Gen 1:4 GNB)
Compassion	*raham* *naham* <u>*splanchnizomai*</u> <u>*eleeō*</u>	A feeling of distress or pity for the suffering or misfortune of others.	Somewhat distinct from love, compassion is often prompted by a specific circumstance.	When he saw the crowds, he **had compassion** (*splanchnizomai*) on them (Mt 9:36).
Love	*hesed* *'ahav* <u>*agapē*</u> <u>*phileō*</u>	An intense emotion of affection, warmth, fondness and regard toward a person or thing.	Love tends to be more lasting than compassion.	I have **loved** (*'ahav*) you with an everlasting **love** (*'ahav*); I have drawn you with **loving-kindness** (*hesed*) (Jer 31:3).

questions for reflection and discussion

THESE QUESTIONS AND SUGGESTIONS could be used either for personal reflection (write, reflect) or for small group discussion (share). Feel free to modify a "write"/"reflect" question to fit a discussion format, or to modify a "share" question to fit a personal reflection setting.

1. EMOTIONS ARE DIVINE

1. Read and pray through Psalm 69, reflecting on the expressions of emotions, both God's and the psalmist's. What did you learn about God? About prayer?

2. Notice your emotions after you read a moving novel or watch a dramatic show. What did you feel? Anger, sorrow, joy? Discuss your emotions with a friend or a small group.

3. Reflect on a moment of pain, crisis, or tragedy in your life. Write a psalm of lament, pouring out your heart to God. Make it emotional and hyperbolic. Share your psalm with a loved one.

4. Since "talking about emotions brings clarity," meet with a friend or a small group to discuss these application questions.

2. THE HATRED OF GOD

1. Why are we so troubled by a description of a God who hates? What is it about God's character that doesn't seem consistent with hatred?

2. If you were in the place of Bonhoeffer, what would you say to Werner von Haeften, if he asked you if he should shoot Hitler? How would you justify your stance?

3. What evil behaviors do you hate? Spend time praying against these actions, usually the language of Psalm 139 as you feel comfortable. Remember to ask God to purify your motives as you pray.

3. THE WRATH OF GOD

1. Where do you feel righteous anger? How can you use it to motivate you toward righteous actions? What can you do this week to respond?

2. Pick a biblical text where God gets angry. Read, reflect, and pray about what motivated his anger. What did you learn about God, his character, and his emotions?

3. How can you take concrete steps in the next week to act on your righteous anger to help people who are often marginalized (immigrants, foreigners, single mothers, children)?

4. THE JEALOUSY OF GOD

1. Which of your relationships are you most likely to feel jealous about? What is it about that relationship that causes you to treasure it, value it, and feel protective about it? How can you let that person (or those people) know how you feel about the relationship in a proactive, healthy, affirming way?

2. How does it affect your relationship with God to know that his love for you is jealous and that he desires your exclusive focus?

3. In what contexts are you jealous for God, jealous that others are exclusively devoted to him? What could you do to help others realize that God jealously desires to be in relationship with them?

5. THE SORROW OF GOD

1. How does it affect you to know that God is grieved over sin, even your sin specifically?

2. Share a time you were deeply sorrowful that someone close to you was in pain. What made it so painful to you? If you haven't done so already, express your grief to your grieving friend.

3. How comfortable do you feel weeping in public? How does it affect you to know that Yahweh in the Old Testament and Jesus in the New wept?

6. THE JOY OF GOD

1. Write down ten things that give you joy. What gave you immense joy recently? Share these joys with other people.

2. What do you find most delightful about Yahweh in the Old Testament? What about Jesus in the New Testament? Why?

3. What aspect of your character do you think God finds the most delightful? Tell someone why you think God is delighted about you.

7. THE COMPASSION OF GOD

1. How has God shown compassion to you this past year? How do you think God felt about extending compassion to you?

2. Whom do you find it easy to show compassion toward? Whom do you find it hard? Why?

3. Reread and reflect on the story of Jesus' healing of the two blind men in Matthew 20:29-34. Who do you most relate to (the crowd, the disciples, the blind men, Jesus)? Why? Would you have persisted if you were the blind men? Why or why not?

8. THE LOVE OF GOD

1. Whether or not you got into an argument (or fight?) with someone recently, copy out by hand 1 Corinthians 13. What did you learn?

2. Share a time in your life when you, like Joseph, were loved by God in an expected place and in an unexpected way.

3. Sometime today sing out loud, loudly (by yourself or with others), "Jesus loves me this I know, for the Bible tells me so . . ." Reflect on the message of this song for you and your loved ones.

4. Pray that God gives you the courage, and love, to speak the truth in love to a person who needs to hear it. Then go do it. Right now.

EPILOGUE

1. In what contexts are you tempted to stifle your emotions? How can you take steps to express emotions more freely in a way that feels genuine and authentic?

2. Which two or three emotions do you sometimes experience simultaneously? How does the realization that God experiences multiple emotions simultaneously help you understand yourself better?

3. Share a story about a time you were emotional in a public setting. How does it feel now to talk about it?

notes

1. EMOTIONS ARE DIVINE

[1] *Brian's Song* was based on the book by Gale Sayers and Al Silverman, *I Am Third* (New York: Viking Press, 1970). Sadly, Gale Sayers passed away while I was writing this book (September 23, 2020).

[2] While some think Martin Luther wrote the carol, it is usually attributed to William J. Kirkpatrick or James Ramsey Murray; https://en.wikipedia.org/wiki /Away_in_a_Manger, accessed September 29, 2021.

[3] Arthur Conan Doyle, *Sign of the Four* (Amazon Classics, 2019), 14, Kindle.

[4] For a longer discussion of the story of Uzzah, see David T. Lamb, *God Behaving Badly: Is the God of the Old Testament Angry, Sexist and Racist?* (Downers Grove, IL: InterVarsity Press, 2022), 31-37.

[5] For more on the topic, see the perspectives of Daniel Castelo, James E. Dolezal, Thomas Jay Oord, and John C. Peckham in *Divine Impassibility: Four Views of God's Emotions and Suffering*, edited by Robert J. Matz and A. Chadwick Thornhill (Downers Grove, IL: IVP Academic, 2019). My own view fits best under either "Qualified Passibility" (Peckham), or "Strong Passibility" (Oord).

[6] For my perspective on the related subject of divine immutability, see "Rigid or Flexible" in *God Behaving Badly*, 139-56, and "The Immutable Mutability of YHWH," *Southeastern Theological Review*, 2.1 (2011): 21-38.

[7] Jack Deere, *Even in Our Darkness: A Story of Beauty in a Broken Life* (Grand Rapids, MI: Zondervan, 2018), 119-20.

[8] Numerous examples of ignoring biblical poetry could be given, but I'll mention two. *The Story: The Bible as One Continuing Story of God and His People* (Grand Rapids, MI: Zondervan, 2011). This version of the story is basically narrative selections from the NIV omitting poetry—Psalms and the vast majority of prophetic literature. Craig G. Bartholomew and Michael W. Goheen, *The Drama of Scripture: Finding Our Place in the Biblical Story* (Grand Rapids, MI: Baker,

2014). While I frequently use *Drama of Scripture* as a textbook, and most students love it, I find it troubling how little emphasis they give to biblical poetry.

[9]David T. Lamb, "Hosea the Book" in *The Baker Illustrated Bible Dictionary*, ed. Tremper Longman III (Grand Rapids, MI: Baker Academic, 2013), 805.

[10]Castelo et al., *Divine Impassibility*, 61.

[11]Walter Brueggemann, "The Recovering God of Hosea," *Horizons in Biblical Theology* 30 (2008): 6.

[12]Merriam-Webster defines *emotions*: "A conscious mental reaction (such as anger or fear) subjectively experienced as strong feeling usually directed toward a specific object and typically accompanied by physiological and behavior changes in the body." *Merriam-Webster's Unabridged Dictionary*, Merriam-Webster, https://unabridged.merriam-webster.com/unabridged/emotion, accessed October 22, 2021.

[13]Daniel Coleman, *Emotional Intelligence: Why It Can Matter More than IQ*, Tenth Anniversary Edition (New York: Bantam, 2005), 289-90. See also Julie Beck, "Hard Feelings: Science's Struggle to Define Emotions," *Atlantic*, February 24, 2015, www.theatlantic.com/health/archive/2015/02/hard-feelings-sciences-struggle-to-define-emotions/385711/.

[14]For a recent, readable work on the science of emotions, see Lisa Feldman Barrett, *How Emotions Are Made: The Secret Life of the Brain* (Boston: Mariner Books, 2018).

[15]C. S. Lewis, *Reflections on the Psalms* (New York: Harcourt Brace Jovanovich, 1958), 95.

[16]Coleman, *Emotional Intelligence*, 28.

[17]Brené Brown discusses eighty-seven emotions that humans experience grouped into thirteen categories. Her list includes all seven of the emotions discussed in this book. She believes that understanding emotions is critical to understanding our lives and our relationships. See *Atlas of the Heart: Mapping Meaningful Connection and the Language of Human Experience* (New York: Random House, 2021).

[18]Aristotle, *Rhetoric*, Book II (Infomotions, Inc., 2000), 41-60, ebook.

[19]Charles Darwin, *The Expressions of the Emotions in Man and Animals* (London: John Murray, 1872), accessed July 20, 2020, Darwin Online.

[20]Robert Plutchik, "The Nature of Emotions," *American Scientist* 89, no. 4 (July–August, 2001): 344-50.

[21]The director of *Inside Out*, Pete Docter, consulted two psychologists who study emotion, Paul Ekman and Dacher Keltner. "It's All in Your Head: Director Pete Docter Gets Emotional in 'Inside Out,'" *Fresh Air*, NPR, accessed July 20, 2020,

www.npr.org/2015/06/10/413273007/its-all-in-your-head-director-pete-docter
-gets-emotional-in-inside-out.

[22]See Peter Krol, "Top 10 OT Books Quoted in NT," Knowable Word, March 20, 2013, www.knowableword.com/2013/03/20/top-10-ot-books-quoted-in-nt/.

[23]I discuss these names in greater depth in *God Behaving Badly*, 22-24.

[24]See John Goldingay, *Psalms: Volume 2: Psalms 42-89* (Grand Rapids, MI: Baker Academic, 2007), 339.

[25]Two other psalms that appear perhaps more frequently in the New Testament than 69 are 22 and 110.

[26]James L. Mays, *Psalms* (Louisville, KY: John Knox Press, 1994), 229.

[27]Goldingay, *Psalms: Volume 2*, 356.

2. THE HATRED OF GOD

[1]Jennifer Chiaverini, *Resistance Women* (New York: William Morrow, 2019), 31, digital version. Three of four primary "resistance women" were real people.

[2]In German, "Heil Hitler! Deutschland erwache! Juda verrecke!"

[3]See Derek Kidner, *Proverbs* (Downers Grove, IL: InterVarsity Press, 1964), 73.

[4]See David T. Lamb, *Prostitutes and Polygamists: A Look at Love, Old Testament Style* (Grand Rapids, MI: Zondervan, 2015), 72-78, 91-101, 146-48.

[5]Various interpretations are given for Jacob's new name "Israel" (e.g., "God strives") but in the context of this story "God-wrestler" makes more sense than "God strives."

[6]In his discussion of Romans 9:13, James D. G. Dunn states, "In Mal 1:2-5, the initiative is entirely God's, without any reference to Esau's (or Edom's) deeds." If Dunn were to focus only on Malachi 1:2-3, I might agree with him, but Malachi 1:4 clearly focuses on their wicked deeds. See James D. G. Dunn, *Romans 9-16* (Grand Rapids, MI: Zondervan, 2018), 544, ebook.

[7]Several New Testament scholars specifically state that the divine hatred in Malachi isn't emotional, but is focused on will and election (Dunn, Michael F. Bird). However, they provide no support for the idea of a hatred devoid of emotions, since there is nothing in Malachi 1 to suggest this. The context of Malachi 1 speaks of not only of hate, but also of love (three times) and wrath (Mal 1:4). Dunn, *Romans 9-16*, 545. Michael F. Bird, *Romans* (Grand Rapids, MI: Zondervan, 2016), 329, ebook.

[8]Gordon Wenham states, "These (imprecatory) psalms teach their users to reflect on their own complicity in and responsibility for violence and oppression" in *Psalms as Torah: Reading Biblical Song Ethically* (Grand Rapids, MI: Baker Academic, 2012), 178.

[9]For example, see Robert H. Mounce, *The Book of Revelation* (Grand Rapids, MI: Eerdmans, 1977), 89.

[10]Adam Hamilton, *Half Truths: God Helps Those Who Help Themselves and Other Things the Bible Doesn't Say* (Nashville, TN: Abingdon Press, 2016), 139-63.

[11]Dietrich Bonhoeffer, *The Extraordinariness of the Christian Life: A Bible Study on the Sermon on the Mount* (New York: National Student Christian Federation, 1964), 45-46.

[12]My primary source for background on Bonhoeffer's resistance to the Nazis is Charles Marsh, *Strange Glory: A Life of Dietrich Bonhoeffer* (New York: Alfred A Knopf, 2014), 184-99. Marsh titles this chapter, "Killing the Madman."

[13]Chiaverini, *Resistance Women*, 448.

[14]The Hate Man passed away in 2017. For his obituary, see Melissa Wen, "Beloved Berkeley 'Hate Man' Dies at 80," *The Daily Californian*, April 3, 2017, www .dailycal.org/2017/04/03/beloved-berkeley-hate-man-dies-80/.

3. THE WRATH OF GOD

[1]David T. Lamb, "Wrath," in *The Dictionary of the Old Testament: Prophets*, eds. Mark J. Boda and J. Gordon McConville (Downers Grove, IL: InterVarsity Press, 2012), 878-83.

[2]David T. Lamb, *God Behaving Badly: Is the God of the Old Testament Angry, Sexist and Racist?* (Downers Grove, IL: InterVarsity Press, 2022), 29-50.

[3]David T. Lamb, "Compassion and Wrath as Motivations for Divine Warfare," in *Holy War in the Bible: Christian Morality and an Old Testament Problem*, eds. H. A. Thomas, J. Evans, and P. Copan (Downers Grove, IL: InterVarsity Press, 2013), 133-51.

[4]Wrath ATX golf clubs are made by Slazenger.

[5]Yoda is addressing Anakin Skywalker in the presence of Jedi Council, "Fear is the path to the dark side . . . fear leads to anger . . . anger leads to hate . . . hate leads to suffering" from *Star Wars: Episode 1, The Phantom Menace*, directed by George Lucas (San Rafael, CA: Lucasfilm, 1999).

[6]Only the first four of these Greek words are used to describe divine anger. Only some of the references listed in the final column involve divine anger. The final three Greek words appear only once in the New Testament.

[7]The master in Matthew 18:34 and in Luke 14:21 represents God in these parables of Jesus.

[8]A. W. Pink, *Attributes of God* (Grand Rapids, MI: Baker, 2006), 106.

[9]This section is full of spoilers, but I don't apologize for spoilers for films over ten years old.

[10] *The Empire Strikes Back*, directed by Irvin Kershner (San Rafael, CA: Lucasfilm, 1980).

[11] *Star Wars: Episode 3, Revenge of the Sith*, directed by George Lucas (San Rafael, CA: Lucasfilm, 2005).

[12] This table focuses only on the Old Testament. We'll get to Jesus and the New Testament later.

[13] John Goldingay states, "God gets angry only as a reaction to outside stimulus," *Old Testament Theology (Volume Two): Israel's Faith* (Downers Grove, IL: IVP Academic, 2006), 141.

[14] See also my discussion of divine anger in Exodus in *God Behaving Badly*, 37-45.

[15] Notable examples from history include the Reign of Terror in France and the Russian Revolution.

[16] For an insightful discussion of the significance of Exodus 34:6-7, see Walter Brueggemann, *Theology of the Old Testament: Testimony, Dispute, Advocacy* (Minneapolis: Fortress, 1997), 215-28.

[17] Martin Luther King Jr., *The Trumpet of Conscience*, Steeler Lecture, Dexter Avenue Baptist Church, Montgomery, Alabama, November 17, 1967.

[18] Aristotle, *Nicomachean Ethics*, ed. W. D. Ross, and trans. L. Brown (Oxford: Oxford University Press, 2009), book 2, 1108b.

[19] John Goldingay, *Psalms, Volume 1* (Grand Rapids, MI: Baker Academic, 2006), 66.

[20] Scot McKnight, "God Behaving Badly 5," *Jesus Creed*, May 31, 2011, www.patheos.com/blogs/jesuscreed/2011/05/31/god-behaving-badly-5/.

4. THE JEALOUSY OF GOD

[1] Felix Just, "New Testament Statistics," Catholic Resources for Bible, Liturgy, Art, and Theology, accessed January 4, 2021, https://catholic-resources.org/Bible/NT-Statistics-Greek.htm.

[2] James O'Donnell, "St. Augustine," *Britannica*, accessed January 4, 2021, www.britannica.com/biography/Saint-Augustine.

[3] Augustine, *Against Adimantus*, chapter XIII, "Of the Worship of Idols," end of section two, accessed April 6, 2022, www.bibliotheque-monastique.ch/biblio theque/bibliotheque/saints/augustin/polemiques/manicheens/adimantus.htm#_Toc27999138.

[4] Mark Cartwright, "Hera," *World History Encyclopedia*, September 10, 2012, www.ancient.eu/Hera/.

[5] The Big Dipper is part of Ursa Major.

[6] William Shakespeare, *Othello*, act 3, scene 3.

[7] The Killers, "Mr. Brightside," *Hot Fuss*, Island - Lizard King, 2003.

[8] If you wonder, *Why not perform at Allegiant Stadium?* I think it had something to do with Covid. The Killers are originally from Las Vegas.

[9] Noam Shpancer, "Jealousy Hurts Love, or Does It?" *Psychology Today*, April 1, 2015, www.psychologytoday.com/us/blog/insight-therapy/201504/jealousy-hurts-love-or-does-it.

[10] Maya Angelou, *Wouldn't Take Nothing for My Journey Now* (New York: Random House, 1993), 129.

[11] In the Bible, divine jealousy and divine wrath often appear together (e.g., Deut 29:20; 32:16, 21; Ps 78:58; 79:5; Zech 8:2).

[12] For a helpful discussion of these terms, see K. Erik Thoennes, *Godly Jealousy: A Theology of Intolerant Love* (Glasgow: Mentor, 2005), 8-16. Thoennes includes a comprehensive list of Hebrew and Greek jealousy terms and their contexts in appendixes two and three, pages 275-77.

[13] On jealousy and envy (definitions of, distinctions between, and discussion of), see Brené Brown, *Atlas of the Heart* (New York: Random House 2021), 25-29.

[14] John Mark McMillan, "How He Loves," *The Song Inside the Sounds of Breaking Down*, John Mark McMillan, 2015.

[15] David T. Lamb, "The 14 Commandments," *David T. Lamb* (blog), accessed February 25, 2021, https://davidtlamb.com/2011/11/02/the-14-commandments/.

[16] David T. Lamb, *God Behaving Badly: Is the God of the Old Testament Angry, Sexist and Racist?* (Downers Grove, IL: InterVarsity Press, 2022), 41-46.

[17] For a discussion of when and why God changes, see "Rigid or Flexible?" in *God Behaving Badly*, 135-52.

[18] There are three troubling incidents of violence in this story, Exodus 34:5-14. God threatens to wipe out his people (Ex 32:10), the Levites kill three thousand of their "brothers" with the sword (Ex 32:26-29), and God sends a plague on the people because of the calf (Ex 32:35). I won't be able to adequately resolve these issues here, but will simply make two points. First, each of these incidents are highly problematic and cannot be easily resolved. Second, the only incident where God actually does something violent is the third one, and we know very little of what the plague involved. See also my discussion of the problem of violence in the Old Testament in *God Behaving Badly*, 97-117.

[19] For a legal definitions of a "crime of passion" or the "heat of passion," see "Crime of Passion," Cornell Law School Legal Information Institute, accessed April 13, 2022, www.law.cornell.edu/wex/crime_of_passion.

[20] Not all English translations reflect these repetitions in the Hebrew, but these two verses could be translated literally as "I am jealous for Jerusalem and for

Zion with great jealousy" (Zech 1:14) and "I am jealous for Zion with great jealousy, and I am jealous for her with great wrath" (Zech 8:2).

21For example, Walter Brueggemann, *Isaiah 1-39* (Louisville, KY: Westminster John Knox, 1998), 84; John N. Oswalt, *Isaiah* (Grand Rapids, MI: Eerdmans, 1998), 248.

22The Jealous Husband law of Numbers 5:11-31 is not explicitly connected to a concern for God or idolatry. While the law seems unfair, within their patriarchal context the law is meant to protect the wife; see David T. Lamb, "Holy Water, Jealous Husbands, and Dropping Uteruses," *David T. Lamb* (blog), accessed August 13, 2021, https://davidtlamb.com/2014/09/17/holy-water-jealous -husbands-and-dropping-uteruses/.

23For more on violence in the Old Testament, specifically involving God, see Lamb, *God Behaving Badly*, 97-117.

24*The Confessions of St. Augustine*, trans. John K. Ryan (Garden City, NY: Doubleday, 1960), 8.6.14. References to his *Confessions* are in the form book. chapter.paragraph.

25*Confessions*, 8.7.17.

26*Confessions*, 8.7.17.

27*Confessions*, 8.11.27.

28*Confessions*, 8.12.28.

29*Confessions*, 8.12.29.

30*Confessions*, 8.12.30.

5. THE SORROW OF GOD

1In chapter six we'll revisit the idea of God's first emotion—I think he displayed emotion in Genesis 1.

2I discuss the ethically troubling nature of the flood narrative in David T. Lamb, *God Behaving Badly* (Downers Grove, IL: InterVarsity Press, 2022) 201-216.

3Christopher Wright, *Deuteronomy* (Peabody, MA: Hendrickson, 1996), 267-68.

4See Lamb, *God Behaving Badly*, 97-117. Also see David T. Lamb, "Reconciling the God of Love with the God of Genocide," *Relevant* 53, September-October 2011, 106-109.

5See for example, Robert Bergen, *1, 2 Samuel* (Nashville, TN: B&H Publishing, 1996), 170.

6See Gen 6:6 ESV, NIV; Gen 6:7 NIV; 1 Sam 15:11 NASB, ESV, NIV, NRSV.

7See Gen 6:6 NASB, NRSV, NLT; Gen 6:7 ESV, NLT; 1 Sam 15:11 NLT. Curiously, as Samuel describes God's character to Saul in the middle of this incident he says God does not change, using the same verb, *naham* (1 Sam 15:29).

[8]These texts may or may not use synonyms for sorrow; see John Goldingay, *Old Testament Theology (Volume Two): Israel's Faith* (Downers Grove, IL: InterVarsity Press, 2006), 130-34.

[9]For a clear argument why the voice associated with these emotional expressions (Is 15:5; 16:9, 11) is God himself, see J. Alec Motyer, *Isaiah: An Introduction & Commentary* (Downers Grove, IL: InterVarsity Press, 1999), 124-30.

[10]Motyer, *Isaiah*, 126.

[11]While some scholars think that the person weeping in Jeremiah 9 and 48 is the prophet or someone else, Fretheim makes a compelling argument from the text that God is the one weeping; Terence E. Fretheim, *Jeremiah* (Macon, GA: Smith & Helwys, 2002), 157-66, 601-605.

[12]See my discussion of this incident, "Changing the Mind of God: The Prayer and Tears of King Hezekiah" in *Speaking with God: Probing Old Testament Prayers for Contemporary Significance*, eds. Phillip G. Camp and Elaine A. Phillips (Eugene, OR: Pickwick, 2021), 66-80.

[13]Charles Gabriel, "I Stand Amazed in the Presence," 1905.

[14]Chris Fenner, "I Stand Amazed in the Presence," Hymnology Archive, accessed June 14, 2021, www.hymnologyarchive.com/i-stand-amazed.

[15]David E. Garland, *Luke* (Grand Rapids, MI, Zondervan, 2011), ebook, accessed June 18, 2021.

[16]Tim Mackie, on his podcast, "Exploring My Strange Bible," thinks Jesus experienced a panic attack in the garden. See Tim Mackie, "Panic Attack," Gospel of Matthew, Part 33, accessed July 5, 2021, https://bibleproject.com/podcast/matthew-p33-panic-attack/.

[17]For the story of Mark Driscoll and his church, see the CT podcast *The Rise and Fall of Mars Hill*. Mike Cosper, "I am Jack's Raging Bile Duct," episode 4, July 14, 2021, in *The Rise and Fall of Mars Hill*, produced by Mike Cosper and *Christianity Today*, podcast, 51:00, www.christianitytoday.com/ct/podcasts/rise-and-fall-of-mars-hill/.

[18]I found this quote in Rachel Held Evans, "Inside Mark Driscoll's Disturbed Mind," *Rachel Held Evans* (blog), July 29, 2014, accessed February 3, 2022, https://rachelheldevans.com/blog/driscoll-troubled-mind-william-wallace.

[19]Most English translations (e.g., ESV, NASB, NIV) render John 11:35 in nine letters, "Jesus wept," but it is much longer in the original Greek, three words, sixteen letters (ἐδάκρυσεν ὁ Ἰησοῦς).

[20]F. F. Bruce, *The Gospel of John* (Grand Rapids, MI: Eerdmans, 1983), 246; and William Hendrickson, *John* (Grand Rapids, MI: Baker Academic, 1953), 155.

[21]Raymond Brown, *The Gospel According to John (I-XII)* (Garden City, NY: Doubleday & Company, 1966), 425; and Bruce, *John*, 246.

[22]Bruce, *John*, 246.

[23]See for example Hendrickson, *John*, 155-56. See also a helpful discussion of this subject by Marianne Meye Thompson, *John: A Commentary* (Louisville, KY: Westminster John Knox, 2015), 249.

6. THE JOY OF GOD

[1]J. M. Sinclair, "Joy," *Collins English Dictionary* (New York: HarperCollins, 1999), 832.

[2]C. S. Lewis, *Letters to Malcolm, Chiefly on Prayer* (New York: Harcourt, 1991), 93.

[3]Jon Favreau, director, *Elf* (Burbank, CA: Warner Bros. Pictures, 2003).

[4]Here are five references linking *tov* and joy: Deut 26:11; Judg 16:25; 2 Chron 6:41; Eccles 2:1; 7:14. Holladay's lexicon gives "joyous, glad" as its first meaning of *tov*; William Lee Holladay and Ludwig Kohler, *A Concise Hebrew Aramaic Lexicon of the Old Testament* (Leiden: Brill, 2000).

[5]The text calls the sun and the moon "the greater light" and "the lesser light" (Gen 1:16).

[6]Walter Brueggemann, *Genesis* (Louisville, KY: Westminster John Knox, 1982), 27.

[7]We aren't sure why whales breach. It might be to play (leaping for joy), but most likely it is to communicate with other whales ("Hey, I'm over here!"—splash!). See Michelle Frey, "Why Do Humpbacks Breach?" *Ocean Conservancy*, April 1, 2020, https://oceanconservancy.org/blog/2020/04/01/humpback-whales -breach/; and Ali Schuler, "Ask the Naturalist: Why Do Whales Breach?" Whale Sense website, accessed October 15, 2021, https://whalesense.org/2020/08/14 /why-do whales-breach/.

[8]J. Alec Motyer, *Isaiah: An Introduction & Commentary* (Downers Grove, IL: InterVarsity Press, 1999), 381.

[9]John Piper discusses Jesus' demand that his followers "rejoice and leap for joy" in *What Jesus Demands from the World* (Wheaton, IL: Crossway, 2006), 83-91. His discussion actively engages with C.S. Lewis and Jonathan Edwards on the topic of joy.

[10]For a more in-depth academic discussion of Jesus' emotions, see F. Scott Spencer, *Passions of the Christ: The Emotional Life of Jesus in the Gospels* (Grand Rapids, MI: Baker Academic, 2021), 229-60 (his chapter on Jesus' joy, "That's Good! The Joyous Jesus").

[11]John the Baptist was also a source of joy for many. Before his birth, the angel told his father, the priest Zechariah, husband of Elizabeth, "He will be a joy and delight to you, and many will rejoice because of his birth" (Lk 1:14).

[12] For a discussion of Old Testament parallels to Mary's song of Luke 1, see Joel B. Green, *The Gospel of Luke* (Grand Rapids, MI: Eerdmans, 1997), 101-102.

[13] Zac Al-Khateeb, "CFB 150: Top 10 Plays in College Football History," Sporting News, October 23, 2019, www.sportingnews.com/us/ncaa-football/news /cfb-150-top-10-plays-in-college-football-history/1tcv3e3tgbt6n11xghvs nbmnya.

[14] According to Stanford fans, two of the Cal laterals were not legal and therefore the touchdown should have been called back. Cal fans disagree.

7. THE COMPASSION OF GOD

[1] Alfred Hitchcock, director, *I Confess* (Burbank, CA: Warner Bros. Pictures, 1953).

[2] J. M. Sinclair, "Compassion," *Collins English Dictionary* (New York: Harper-Collins, 1999), 326.

[3] See John Goldingay's discussion of "Motherly Compassion" in *Old Testament Theology (Volume Two): Israel's Faith* (Downers Grove, IL: IVP Academic, 2006), 112-13.

[4] See also my discussion, David T. Lamb, "Compassion and Wrath as Motivations for Divine Warfare," in *Holy War in the Bible: Christian Morality and an Old Testament Problem*, eds. H. A. Thomas, J. Evans, and P. Copan (Downers Grove, IL: InterVarsity Press, 2013), 133-51.

[5] See the discussion of this formulaic description of God in Terence E. Fretheim, *Exodus* (Louisville, KY, Westminster John Knox, 2010), 301-302.

[6] Darran Simon, "Botham Jean's Brother Hugs the Former Police Officer Who Killed Him," CNN, October 3, 2019, https://edition.cnn.com/2019/10/02/us /botham-jean-brother-amber-guyger-hug/index.html.

[7] In the film, this dialogue is set in the mines of Moria, while in the book it is set much earlier at Frodo's home (with Sam outside the window "eavesdropping"— even though there are no eaves around to be dropped); J. R. R. Tolkien, *The Fellowship of the Ring* (New York: Mariner Books, 1994), 58. While we lived in Oxford, Tolkien's home, we had a delightful time in the spring of 2006 hosting his daughter, Priscilla Tolkien, for tea at our home. We had been warned to not ask about the films, so she regaled us with stories of her father's writing.

[8] *The Lord of the Rings: The Fellowship of the Ring*, directed by Peter Jackson (Burbank, CA: New Line Cinema, 2001).

[9] Here are more examples of God responding with favor to rulers evaluated as evil: Solomon (1 Kings 3:5-12; 11:6), Jeroboam (1 Kings 13:6; 14:9), and Ahab (1 Kings 16:30; 21:27-29).

[10] While many preachers and scholars call what David did with Bathsheba adultery, the textual evidence is stronger that it was a power rape; see my discussion of the incident in David T. Lamb, *Prostitutes and Polygamists: A Look at Love, Old Testament Style* (Grand Rapids, MI: Zondervan, 2015), 127-34.

[11] David was the second most popular boy name in the United States in the year of my birth (1962): "Most Popular Baby Names of 1962," BabyCenter website, accessed October 21, 2021, www.babycenter.com/baby-names/most-popular/top-baby-names-1962.

[12] See my discussion of Mark's version of this story (Mk 7:24-30) in David T. Lamb, *God Behaving Badly: Is the God of the Old Testament Angry, Sexist and Racist?* (Downers Grove, IL: InterVarsity Press, 2022), 151-55.

[13] The title "The Good Samaritan" is problematic since it suggests that Samaritans were not generally "good." If you're from the United States, how would you feel about a story titled "The Good American"? A better title for the parable might be "The Outrageously Compassionate Samaritan" or "Like a Good Neighbor, the Samaritan Was There."

8. THE LOVE OF GOD

[1] My mom preferred the Good News Bible (Today's English Version); she was a volunteer for the American Bible Society, which publishes it. I still use it in my daily devotions in memory of Mom.

[2] J. M. Sinclair, "Love," *Collins English Dictionary* (New York: HarperCollins, 1999), 919.

[3] I, however, ask "How does one reconcile the loving God of the Old Testament with the harsh God of the New Testament?" in David T. Lamb, *God Behaving Badly: Is the God of the Old Testament Angry, Sexist and Racist?* (Downers Grove, IL: InterVarsity Press, 2022), 13.

[4] Michael Card wrote an entire book on *hesed*: *Inexpressible: Hesed and the Mystery of God's Lovingkindness* (Downers Grove, IL: InterVarsity Press, 2018).

[5] Lamb, *God Behaving Badly*, 42.

[6] C. S. Lewis, *The Four Loves* (San Francisco: HarperOne, 2017; originally published in 1960 by Harcourt Brace).

[7] Although, the antonym of *storgē* (*astorgos* "unloving") appears twice (Rom 1:31; 2 Tim 3:3), and a compound form with *philia* (*philostorgos* "loving dearly") appears once (Rom 12:10).

[8] People mentioned God's *hesed* in their prayers earlier (Gen 24:12, 27; 32:10).

[9] See also John Goldingay, *Psalms: Volume 1: Psalms 1–41* (Grand Rapids, MI: Baker, 2006), 352.

[10] See "15 of the Fastest Dog Breeds in the World," Highland Canine website, January 31, 2021, https://highlandcanine.com/the-fastest-dog-breeds-in-the -world/.

[11] Peter Krol ranks Leviticus 19:18 as the top Old Testament verse quoted most in the New Testament in this blog: Peter Krol, "Top 11 OT Verses Quoted in NT," *Knowable Word* (blog), April 10, 2013, www.knowableword.com/2013/04/10 /top-10-ot-verses-quoted-in-nt/.

[12] Jesus makes a few changes to the list of the Ten Commandments (Ex 20:12-17; Deut 5:16-21). He puts the honoring parents command at the end and changes "do not covet" to "do not defraud."

[13] Here is his obituary "Richard C. Lamb," *Physics Today*, May 12, 2018, https:// physicstoday.scitation.org/do/10.1063/pt.6.4o.20180512a/full/.

EPILOGUE

[1] So, not really "the age of women."

[2] *The Crown*, season 4, episode 2, "The Balmoral Test," directed by Paul Whittington, written by Peter Morgan, aired November 15, 2020, on Netflix.

[3] I am not suggesting that the Bible is the only resource one should read to understand emotions. I have mentioned many other references throughout this book (I'll mention two more in this conclusion), but I will highlight two here that I have found particularly helpful. From the perspective of counselor and an biblical scholar, see Dan B. Allender and Tremper Longman III, *The Cry of the Soul: How Our Emotions Reveal Our Deepest Questions about God* (Colorado Springs, CO: NavPress, 1994). For a popular introduction to the science of emotions, see Daniel Coleman, *Emotional Intelligence: Why It Can Matter More than IQ* (New York: Bantam Books, 2006).

[4] Chip Heath and Dan Heath, *Made to Stick: Why Some Ideas Survive and Others Die* (New York: Random House, 2007, 2008); pages 165-203 focus on emotions.

[5] James M. Lang, *Small Teaching: Everyday Lessons from the Science of Learning* (San Francisco: Jossey-Bass, 2016), 167-93.

[6] Heath, *Made to Stick*, 227-29.

[7] Lang, *Small Teaching*, 182.

[8] Lang, *Small Teaching*, 192.

[9] I will not be able to do justice to the doctrine of the divine incarnation adequately with a brief reference, but perhaps John 1:1-18 is the one text that does it best.

[10] Hope (Psalm 119:43, 74, 81, 114, 116, 147, 166); affliction (Psalm 119:50, 67, 71, 75, 92, 107, 153); longing (Psalm 119:20, 40, 81, 82, 123, 131, 174); heart (Psalm 119:2, 7, 10, 11, 32, 34, 36, 58, 69, 70, 80, 111, 112, 145, 161).

for further reading

Allender, Dan B. and Tremper Longman, III. *The Cry of the Soul: How Our Emotions Reveal Our Deepest Questions about God.* Colorado Springs: NavPress, 2015.

Barrett, Lisa Feldman. *How Emotions Are Made: The Secret Life of the Brain.* Boston: Mariner Books, 2018.

Brown, Brené. *Atlas of the Heart.* New York: Random House, 2021.

Brueggemann, Walter. *Theology of the Old Testament.* Minneapolis: Fortress, 1997.

Coleman, Daniel. *Emotional Intelligence: Why It Can Matter More than IQ.* Tenth Anniversary Edition. New York: Bantam, 2005.

Goldingay, John. *Old Testament Theology (Volume Two): Israel's Faith.* Downers Grove, IL: InterVarsity Press, 2006.

Goldingay, John. *Psalms, Volume 1: Psalms 1–41; Volume 2: Psalms 42–89; Volume 3: Psalms 90–150.* Grand Rapids, MI: Baker Academic, 2006, 2007, 2008.

Heath, Chip and Dan Heath. *Made to Stick: Why Some Ideas Survive and Others Die.* New York: Random House, 2007, 2008.

Lamb, David T. "Changing the Mind of God: The Prayer and Tears of King Hezekiah." In *Speaking with God: Probing Old Testament Prayers for Contemporary Significance*, edited by Phillip G. Camp and Elaine A. Phillips, 66-80. Eugene, OR: Pickwick, 2021.

Lamb, David T. "Compassion and Wrath as Motivations for Divine Warfare." In *Holy War in the Bible: Christian Morality and an Old Testament Problem*, edited by H. A. Thomas, J. Evans, and P. Copan, 133-51. Downers Grove, IL: InterVarsity Press, 2013.

Lamb, David T. *God Behaving Badly: Is the God of the Old Testament Angry, Sexist and Racist*, expanded edition. Downers Grove, IL: InterVarsity Press, 2022.

Lamb, David T. *Prostitutes and Polygamists: A Look at Love, Old Testament Style.* Grand Rapids, MI: Zondervan, 2015.

Lamb, David T. "Wrath." In *Dictionary of the Old Testament: Prophetic Books*, edited by Mark J. Boda and J. Gordon McConville, 878-83. Downers Grove, IL: InterVarsity Press, 2012.

Lang, James M. *Small Teaching: Everyday Lessons from the Science of Learning*. San Francisco: Jossey-Bass, 2016.

Lewis, C. S. *The Four Loves*. San Francisco: HarperOne, 2017.

Marsh, Charles. *Strange Glory: A Life of Dietrich Bonhoeffer*. New York: Alfred A. Knopf, 2014.

Matz, Robert J., and A. Chadwick Thornhill, eds. *Divine Impassibility: Four Views of God's Emotions and Suffering*. Downers Grove, IL: InterVarsity Press, 2019.

Sinclair, J. M., General Consultant. *Collins English Dictionary*. New York: Harper-Collins, 1999.

Spencer, F. Scott. *Passions of the Christ: The Emotional Life of Jesus in the Gospels*. Grand Rapids, MI: Baker Academic, 2021.

Thoennes, K. Erik. *Godly Jealousy: A Theology of Intolerant Love*. Glasgow: Mentor, 2005.

Wenham, Gordon. *Psalms as Torah: Reading Biblical Song Ethically*. Grand Rapids, MI: Baker Academic, 2012.

scripture index

also by david lamb

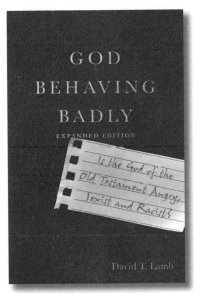

God Behaving Badly
978-1-5140-0349-7